BURNS SINGER

BURNS SINGER

SELECTED POEMS

edited by
Anne Cluysenaar

Carcanet · Manchester

Acknowledgements:

The editor expresses special thanks to Dr Marie Singer and Mr G. S. Fraser for their help in preparing this *Selected Poems*. Some of the poems reprinted here first appeared in the following periodicals and anthologies: *Botteghe Oscure, Encounter, Lines Review, The Listener, New Poems 1955, Poetry Now* (Faber), *Points, The Saltire Review, The Times Literary Supplement*. Many of them were included in *Collected Poems* (1970).

First published in 1977 by
Carcanet New Press Limited
330 Corn Exchange
Manchester M4 3BG

The publisher acknowledges the financial assistance of the Arts Council of Great Britain.

Printed in England
by Unwin Brothers Limited at the Gresham Press, Old Woking

CONTENTS

PREFACE

James Burns Singer was born in New York City on August
29, 1928. His father was born in Manchester, a second-
generation Jewish immigrant from Poland, and his mother in
Scotland. She was of Irish, Scottish and Norwegian background and Burns was her maiden name, later assumed by her
son. He lived most of his life in Britain and died suddenly, of
heart trouble, in Plymouth on 8 September 1964. His ashes
were scattered at sea, but there is a memorial to him in the
churchyard of St Mary the Less (Little St Mary's) in Cambridge.

After the age of four, Singer spent his childhood and early
youth in Scotland, attending school in Glasgow. There is a
diary, begun when he was fifteen, which shows already well-
developed and original literary interests. Between two periods
at Glasgow University, studying first English and then Zoology,
he went to Cornwall to work near W. S. Graham, and then
travelled and worked for several years in Europe. Following
the suicide of his mother, Singer's second period at university
came to an end and he spent four years in Aberdeen as an
assistant in the Marine Laboratory, pursuing both scientific
and literary interests until he left for London in 1955. Once
there, he earned his living by writing, broadcasting, and preparing several books: *Still and All*, a volume of verse which
was the Poetry Book Society Recommendation for 1957;
Living Silver, a documentary novel on the fishing trade, published in the same year; and a selection of translations, *Five
Centuries of Polish Poetry*, with Jerzy Peterkiewicz, published in 1960 and reprinted six years after his death with
the addition of translations by Jerzy Peterkiewicz and Jon
Stallworthy.

Singer's critical, documentary and fictional prose, now
scattered amongst newspapers and periodicals and much of it
still in manuscript, has yet to be collected and published. The
Collected Poems, edited by W. A. S. Keir in 1970 with a preface by Hugh MacDiarmid, omitted a good deal of the verse,
including 'S. O. S. Lifescene', and is now generally unobtain-
able. The present selection is based largely on *Collected Poems*
but includes 'S. O. S. Lifescene' and several poems from

amongst those that remained in his papers. For these, and for the prose passages quoted in the introduction, I am indebted to the poet's widow, Dr Marie Singer, whose help and kindness have been inexhaustible. This selection has been planned to provide the reader with a coherent and poetically valuable nucleus from which the direction and significance of Singer's work may be appreciated. In keeping with this intention, the introduction is devoted to a discussion of Singer's vision rather than of his personal life. The reader who is interested in the latter will wish to turn to the rather detailed biographical material in the *Collected Poems*.

A few years before he died at the age of thirty-six, Singer moved to Cambridge with his wife Marie, whom he married in 1956, and was again engaged in scientific research, this time at the Marine Biology laboratory at Plymouth. Although his poetic development was certainly cut short, the poems brought together here show him to be a poet of importance for the future development of British, and it may be of all, poetry. His creative and intellectual work related and made vital areas of experience nowadays often assumed to be inimical, but which must I believe be brought into conjunction if poetry is to attain a mature, justifiable confidence amongst modern man's other significant activities. I doubt if there is any other writer of the century who offers so much, in this particular way, to creative artists seeking a direction.

INTRODUCTION

I carry that which I am carried by.
The Gentle Engineer

WHEN Burns Singer's first book of poems, *Still and All* (1957), was recommended by the Poetry Book Society, he wrote a short response, part of which reads:

Most forms of composition can be achieved by an urbane and intelligent attachment to the facts of life and the rules of grammar. But, in poetry, grammar ceases to exist and the facts to matter. The poet is landed with the task of creating an autonomous system of rules parallel to those of grammar and of inter-related images that reflect, by an unknown process, both the facts and their transformation, through one another and beyond any of them, into the kind of meaning that used to be called spiritual.

I am sorry if this sounds complicated. Yet I hope it does, because poetry is complicated and a great deal of harm can be done by pretending it is simple. Milton, on the other hand, was right when he said that poetry should be simple—as *Paradise Lost* is simple—but this simplicity must be arrived at by a very devious route or it will not be poetry. On this route it is easy to get lost in an experiential and metaphysical jungle. And it is frightening to be lost. That is another reason why writing poetry frightens me. It is none the less necessary that somebody should arrive at a simple spiritual statement—and that is why I risk getting lost.

As one gets deeper into Singer's poetry, the accuracy of these remarks as a description of his own poetic temper becomes movingly evident. His interests in poetry and biology lead him on into linguistics, philosophy and the philosophy of science. His search was always for a view of the universe in which man, and his linguistic and intellectual activities, could be seen to have what Wallace Stevens might have called a 'noble' role. For Singer such a view, if it was to be attained at all, must be attained without intellectual or emotional compromise. Although his poetry is the best representation of his life's effort, the notebooks and essays, published and unpublished, in which he recorded his explorations, afford valuable insights into what was indeed a complicated process of simplification. The reader needs help with Singer's ways of thinking because of the originality of their poetic implications. In 'Open Letter to a Critic' (printed in *Twentieth Century*) he wrote that

> knowledge, though it has been increasing at an alarming rate, has not been becoming increasingly atomised as is sometimes supposed by journalists. On the contrary, the various fields of knowledge are coming into ever closer relationships [. . .]. The literary artist, the ventriloquist's doll through which all human conscience should speak, can no longer think of an entity called human life as his subject and dismiss most of real human life, the sciences and technicalities, as so many discrete specialities. [. . .] As the net of unassimilated knowledge tightened until the writer found that most of his life was conditioned by things he could not express, it became imperative for him to enlarge his own language to include more and more of the ways of life that had been created in his absence. [. . .] The present breach in human consciousness, in an age when our physical power is almost absolute, could easily prove fatal.

The literary scene in Britain is still such as to offer considerable resistance to this approach, and it is difficult for writers to develop responses adequate, in Singer's terms, to the demands of contemporary life, capable of closing the gap between physical and spiritual power. Nevertheless, even in a more traditional view of the poet's role, it must be wrong to ignore scientific investigations which, as Singer wrote in another piece for *Twentieth Century*, 'are changing not only the structure of the world around us but the way in which our minds work'. The poet must not merely respond to the universe and himself in ways consistent with scientific discoveries, but must 'adapt his language to the processes of scientific thinking'.

It would be a mistake to suppose that Singer's emphasis on science indicates that science was for him more important than poetry. On the contrary, poetry, as the most vital communicative use of language, appeared to him to take place on the cutting edge of human consciousness. But he knew that the greatest challenge to our faith in this act of communication—so great a challenge that, almost since Keats's realisation of it, poets have ceased to face it at all—comes from science. Or rather, from the uncreative scientist's and non-scientist's misunderstanding of science, and indeed of poetry, as human activities. Like Keats, whose thought Singer's often resembles (not least in its toughness), he knew that knowledge was necessary to ease the burden of the mystery. In what follows, I sketch Singer's main insights into the crisis in communication which has been with us now for almost a century, and of the poet's role as 'ventriloquist'. But ultimately, of course, it is the poems that will speak for him and for us. They are at once sophisticated and natural, and they combine some of the finest qualities of romantic and classical writing. The reader needs no literary background to approach them. Even a poem like 'The Coming of the Grain', which has been singled out by reviewers as difficult, can be read by anyone whose mind is attuned to Singer's modes of perception. The insights afforded by scientific exploration, and the habits of mind it engenders, are every bit as fascinating as those of fantasy. And in the present situation, why pay a witch when what we need is an engineer?

One approach to Singer's world is through his involvement with the sea. As a marine biologist, his research was into the environment and food of the marine organisms that serve as food to the fish we eat. In other words his scientific and imaginative involvement was with the life-engendering and life-giving interaction of organisms with each other. And with the sea, understood literally or metaphorically. In *Living Silver*, the former is central, while in his poetry it is the latter of which we are more aware, even when the sea is (as it is often) also literally present.

> How then did we ever arrive
> (In the house with the hill under it, under us held
> Together by staples and stones, cemented; nailed
> Against one another, and driven against one another)
> arrive
> Alone in the open sea?
> The humped back of a whale, salt bodies we drive

In a hot spurt out of us into insensitive
Air where they stagger like ninepins together, while
                                        separate we
Sink back into the wave.
It drives over us, drives us on under it down.
Then swims slowly, sleepwalking the ocean, to drown
In its own white hair: and drowns us and leaves us with
                                        nothing to save
But bodies built in wet skin.
I do not know whether all this can deprive
Us of dry land, a house, the stubble, where love
Moves like a farmer and staggers and knows his parks to
                                        the bone
And lets harvest arrive.

There are several versions of this poem. It is probably in a rough state, but it does embody the enhancing sense of fear and wonder Singer associates with the sea and with the unknown in emotional and intellectual exploration. His greatest horror is the flat world of cliché and false certainty, of social assurance and spiritual claustrophobia. An adjective he uses often, of both love and landscape, is 'deep'. Life, to reach the fullness of its promise, must lay beings open, must make them permeable to all that is not themselves, must be an extreme risk and yet must genuinely seek not destruction but a greater capacity for experience, a juster understanding of itself and of its own value. Men must be 'capillaries of event'. As he conveys life in 'The Gentle Engineer', from which this phrase comes, it is a progress 'against and over/And off through it towards . . .' If this entails 'the sacrifice bitterly endless of all that man means', as he writes elsewhere, nevertheless it is the only way of being alive, there is no other valid choice.

Language is important to Singer because it is our continual and close environment. He seeks an understanding of it which will show it to be more than a means of commenting on existence, more than a 'tool' we use. Hence his interest in Wittgenstein's philosophical enquiries into the relationship between language and reality, an interest which has been lamented by some of his critics and fellow poets as a false trail. The opinion that an imaginative writer should avoid any hard thinking reflects the intellectual poverty of our present literary culture and has resulted in creative poverty. No question, after all, could be of greater importance to a poet or, for that matter, to any man. It touches on the way in which we understand our relationship with all we perceive, 'within' and 'outside' ourselves, and also on the degree of communication with other beings of which we believe ourselves capable and which we therefore try to attain. The second of these questions is the central subject-matter of linguistics rather than of philosophy, and here again Singer's interest is informed, practical and urgent.

Any brief summary of his conclusions must of course be inadequate, but they amount to a negation of the subject-object dichotomy. He would have agreed with the linguist William Haas that neither philosophical nor linguistic sense can be made of the notion of 'facts uninvolved in language'. As far as human beings are concerned—and can we be concerned further?—facts cannot be observed independently of the senses and of natural and scientific languages. We react to what we perceive through these media. To disentangle 'ourselves' from 'the rest' is impossible. Even colours, for example, are perceived according to the linguistic terms available to define them, and if this is true of such an apparently basic sense-perception, what of the far more complex perceptions and intellections on which human life is based? But Singer throws a fresh light on this approach by his emphasis on man's biological and physical nature. To him, we do not appear as 'over against' nature but as 'part of' it: we are atoms and molecules become seeing and articulate, a man is an eye *of* as well as *on* the universe; he is not isolated or lost, though the process of understanding his true nature may indeed be frightening because it is so unfamiliar, unsanctioned by traditional religious ideas. It is in this sense that 'I carry that which I am carried by', and 'The Gentle Engineer' (of which this is the central theme) draws, in its final long lyric, a beautiful and fragile connection between human love, the seeking out of another being's reality, and man's search for 'knowledge of genesis', of the creative basis of existence:

   . . . you with me
  As I at last

With you, alive
Past apprehension,
The dizzy annunciation, the slackening tension.
In lovemaking there is such a moment, but in the search for
another form of birth, the principle of creation, there may be
no such moment *in life*. The meanings of 'apprehension' are
consummated.

Of the sequence 'Sonnets for a Dying Man', in which father
and son or older and younger man (the present and the future) confront one another, Singer said in a broadcast: 'In
spite of all the vagaries of modern life and philosophy I say
that both life and death are meaningful. I want, that is, to
make an affirmation, an affirmation and not an assertion, and
I want to make it in the context of all our knowledge and of
all we merely think we know'. The manner of these poems
is, for me at least, that of a commentator, and they require to
be read slowly, expanded in the reader's thoughts and related
to the reader's past experience. Their mode seems to be less
in keeping with their ultimate message than does the mode of
'The Gentle Engineer', in which we are offered an actual experience rather than the record of an experience: the reader
does not, here, face the poet so much as stand beside him and
live with him, an experience of sharing rather than of con-
frontation. In this sharing of experience between human
beings there should, as Singer says in 'Words Made of Water',
be 'only darkness, quite anonymous'. Reading such a meditation, one is a participant rather than a receiver, and at times
there is even the impression that the language that is the me-
dium of this experience has reached beyond the relatively
fixed values of lexicon and grammar, the elements of the
language code. Hugh MacDiarmid, in his preface to the
Collected Poems, corrected his first attempt at defining
Singer's style, as 'not words but ectoplasm', in this way:

It was something even stronger than that, and not at all
formless or lacking in development. It affected me as if
someone were talking to me with great urgency in a language I did not understand—a language coming from
whence I had no idea at all. It was clear that Singer and
I were not on the same wave-length, and even now the
poems in his only published volume, *Still and All*, affect

me as if they were spoken by a visitor from outer space—not a 'little green man' arriving from a flying saucer. There was nothing green about Singer at all. Nor did these poems present any of the barriers to understanding of much modern verse—recondite vocabulary, extreme allusiveness, purely private (personal) reference of various kinds. On the contrary. 'Still waters run deep'—Singer's poems had a full even flow of depth I never fathomed, and came from a source I was quite unable to pin-point.

This description captures, despite its reservations, the truly key aspects of Singer's typical manner, its non-literariness, non-privateness, 'depth' and 'impetus', and above all the fact that it constitutes a 'language', which a listener like Mac-Diarmid was prepared to trust even when he could not understand. Interestingly, this account accords with Singer's own description of how poetic language should work. It *should* fail to make sense except for a reader 'on the right wavelength'. The reason for this is worth following up since it has interesting implications.

In several essays and notes, Singer attempted to state clearly why poetry should be 'undefinable'. He insists on the exact phrase, for he does not mean to say that poetry cannot be defined. On the contrary, he defines it *as* 'undefinable', in the sense that it will not allow the reader to decode its utterances as he does those of ordinary language. Of course, he acknowledges that poetic language must preserve certain connections with everyday speech and the language code: we could not grasp it if it did not. However, having emphasised by means of a quotation from Wittgenstein, that 'colloquial language is part of the human organism and no less complex than it', he goes on to comment on the a-logicality and yet insightfulness of many of the comments made on poetry by poets, as against the logical and intelligent but relatively unilluminating comments to be found in 'the more orderly pages of the critics'. Taking Shakespeare and Shelley as examples, he suggests that they are perhaps not *trying* to be logical. Can this be because they have insight into a-logical modes of expression which are nevertheless valid as communication? Perhaps there is 'an a-logical way of using words and that this may be valid in certain situations' and therefore 'no compunction to be logical upon anyone who uses a living language'? In handwritten notes he further suggests that poetry

> exists as or within terms of reference, analogous to dimensions, which are to be found only within the sociological-physiological phenomenon of an individual man or woman, and there is no term of reference by which such a phenomenon can define itself—except of course through its own life, not of course its life as history, as sociology, as relationships, as biology, but its life as an entirety, as a life.

These are jottings not polished for publication, but the drift is clear enough. Man may have an innate biological capacity which allows him to grasp the meaning of language even when it passes beyond socially established values. Whether complete sense can be made of this remains to be seen. Linguists do, however, encounter difficulties when they attempt to account for our understanding of un-grammatical and un-lexical utterances, and when they attempt to explain how language changes. It is one thing to make finer and finer analyses of 'synchronic language states' and to relate different states to each other chronologically. It is another to feel that a really adequate explanation of language-change has been given, or that we know how deviant utterances are grasped in any individual's ever-changing environments. Singer was exploring the notion, partly borrowed from his biological research, that:

> if, instead of attempting to analyse the most complex and highly organised phenomena which we associate with the word 'language', we pass our eyes over some of the simpler phenomena, so simple indeed that they can hardly be dignified by the same name but which yet perform the same biological function of effecting communication between members of the same species, I think we find certain hints as to the original nature of language as a phenomenon, hints which are vastly at variance with our more sophisticated notions of systematic symbolism. At the outset, then, there is that shapeless kinaesthesia that we may imagine to underlie the convergence, after meiosis, of the nuclei of two a-cellular organisms. That some

kinaesthesia is probably present follows from the facts that this sort of copulation takes place, very sporadically, in any environmental conditions which are, in other respects, reasonably favourable for the development of these little animals and that as many as two hundred generations of meiotic division may have intervened in both the participants since their ancestors acted in a similar fashion. Since also meiosis has never been observed to take place except under circumstances (i.e. the presence of another a-cellular organism of the same species which is also undergoing meiosis) which favour copulation it seems very likely that some controlling interaction between the two individuals is a condition of the process.

(Here, incidentally, the sexual metaphor of 'The Gentle Engineer' is given a basis in scientific speculation.) It is not surprising to find Singer elsewhere considering a similar explanation of the 'meaning' of music. His emphasis, in another handwritten note, is on the 'active quality of language. Symbolism static. Language is a symbolism in which the symbols are constantly changing their meaning and their mode of operation. The more they do this the more accurately they reflect the flickering receptivity of the entire human receptor.' For him,

there is a basic inconsistency between the system of language (i.e. grammar, syntax, pronunciation, spelling, etc.) and the function which it is meant to serve (i.e. the communication of the a-systematic world of immediate experience). And this inconsistency penetrates through everything that comes within my concept of language.

From all this it must be clear that the kind of poetry Singer envisages operates on the edge of coded language and verges on silence. To become 'communication' it must be understood by another human being. 'Whereof one cannot speak', in Wittgenstein's famous phrase, thereof a *poet cannot* be silent. His business might be indicated in Emerson's words:

we now and then detect in nature slight dislocations, which apprise us that this surface on which we stand is not fixed, but sliding. These manifold tenacious qualities, this chemistry of vegetation, these metals and animals, which seem to stand there for their own sake, are means and method only, are words of God, and as fugitive as other words.

These are not quite Singer's terms, but the poet, as he sees him, is concerned with sensing such 'dislocations' and attempting to speak their language. Hence, perhaps, the comfort he draws from the ultimate inadequacy of language.

> I have seen words,
> Seen them with thanks, too, shivering, become
> Fragile and useless, pale as the steel sparks
> Tramcars make waifs of when they round a corner.

There is a sense here of directions beyond language, of the mind 'rounding a corner'. In a radio discussion with John Holloway, Donald Davie, D. D. Raphael and Bernard Williams ('Dark Sayings', transmitted June 1957), Singer proposed the riddle as the model of poetry. The genuine poem is a riddle *without* an answer. It is open to its true meaning or to silence, but its meaning can only exist within the right reader. Such poetry is not personal or subjective, it is on the contrary the most exact means of interpersonal communication imaginable. Alvarez, in his review of *Still and All*, was quite wrong to see in the book 'not so much sensitive poems as poems about the difficulties of being sensitive'. Singer's pursuit cannot be seen in such personal terms. His dislike of literary coteries, of accepted styles, is not a matter of romantic individualism. Nor is his rejection of the notion of 'competence' in writing. A writer must be after so difficult a meaning that his language shows the strain. In 'These Poets and You People' he writes:

> It has become fashionable to be a 'good' writer, a perfectionist. In the current jargon, this is called being 'competent'. Have any of its prophets seen it in action? Have they read a poem, and been moved by it, and then found it to be competent? Is *Don Juan* competent? Is *Paradise Lost* or *King Lear*? Of course, they're not. Schoolboys can tear them to pieces in exam papers. And how do we know when a poem is competent? I dare to suggest that it is only when it does not let us catch a glimpse of that reality which words themselves are incompetent to embody, when it shoulders us off with words, when it does

not make us aware of the failure implicit in poetry's attempt at the impossible, when the writer is just not trying, when he is lazy or sterile or plain insensitive. That is competence, and its a bore. Surely it would be better if we all had a chance to have some fun, to see a little life.

He makes the same points in a longer piece entitled 'In Defiance of Dons', where his genuine admiration for and distrust of the young academics of the fifties are equally apparent. In the end, however much we value good writing, the greatest responsibility a poet owes language is to make it enhance life, and a 'finnicking attention to every syllable' is not the way of major poets, who are 'notoriously incompetent'. And, of course, gloriously competent at their true job.

This attitude should not be misinterpreted as slovenliness. Singer's respect for his reader is absolute. He never provides us arrogantly with the outpourings of his subconscious. His respect for modern English, too, is absolute and hopeful:

For the next couple of centuries, at any rate, wooliness should find no place in English and American literature. But unlike any generation between our own and Shakespeare's we have a free but fibred syntax, along with concepts, values and moral evaluations which have never yet received literary expression.

His own attention to detail when he rewrites (he rejects the term 'revision' as a misrepresentation of the process as he knows it) is admirable. Although this is not the place for detailed examples, the reader familiar with 'The Gentle Engineer' will appreciate the semantic implications of the following changes:

The principles of matter ~~are united~~ find each other:
This flake and I converge from ~~emptiness~~ all beginnings.

or

For I no longer know who moves ~~or~~ nor why
~~Nor do my~~ More than my nerves know what they tell my
eye

or

~~A nerve~~ An impulse in an enormous
Structure of round white light
I spin ~~away from touches slight~~ off through it at
The touch of rock, the touch ~~of~~

Of this street, ~~towards towards towards~~ against and over
~~And never reach an end. Towards towards towards . . .~~
And off through it towards . . .

Not only do they render meanings more exact, but they embody the feel of an experience, making mere commentary ('and never reach an end') redundant. Singer's aim is above all kinaesthetic. He would like to 'feel' psychological space, to move in it, to know the depth and motion of a mode of existence in which feeling and thinking cannot be separated. For thought is always and only thought:

The thinking's different: thinking's in the blood . . .

('Oracle Engraved on the Back of a Mirror',
Collected Poems)

And to have confidence, through the experience of the poem itself, that human beings can *meet* in that space. This is of profound moral significance, because

from science itself no man can become aware of the significance, the why, of science. That is to say, science is interested only in the how question. But the wonder of life and the terror of death are incommensurable and irrelevant to all factual data. Therefore science avoids them, but the scientist cannot. And unless a man feel somehow that his life is significant he is unlikely to set much store by how he lives it. [. . .] he will not feel that he is wasting anything.

In the context of these thoughts, Singer's admiration of Milton is immediately comprehensible. Milton, as he wrote in a long eulogy, 'is packed with meaning and it is all personal, not peculiar to his own personality, but peculiar to each of our personalities'. It is in this sense that he understands the true value of the 'grand manner'.

We must always remember what most living poets forget: that poetry is *not* made out of words but rather that, even biologically, the words, their meanings and prime associations, are created by poetry, that poetry *is* the meaning of words for a culture as its economics is the meaning of money, and that it is always a dangerous development when specialised prose or the meaningless jumble which we have made of conversation takes the place of language, that fundamental process of speech, that communication between several entities no matter on what plane of being, which, because of its comprehensive precision, can only and always be called the grand manner.

Singer is interested in language not because he is a poet but because he is a man. His way of writing, 'the way I have of being what I say' as he put it in a notebook, is found rather than sought. After Singer's death, the philosopher John Wisdom wrote to his widow:

Marie, when I have been feeling bad sometimes other people have made things worse for me by trying to take my mind to what is not bad, what is still good in the situation. They have hindered my looking straight and hard at what is bad in the situation. You know that this was not Jimmy's way of meeting what happens in life. His way was to look at what is bad, to look with all the force of his heart and head. . . . Jimmy's way was to look at things, people, situations, with all the force at his disposal at the time, even if this meant getting a distorted view, which required much correction the following morning.

It is this uncompromising search for truth *in living* that lies behind Singer's statement in a notebook: 'to write a poem which does not contain a line of poetry—that would be the great accomplishment'. 'Poetry', here, as against the use of the term in the passage about the grand manner, is the 'poetry' which Eliot declared 'does not matter'.

Perhaps it is precisely because of Singer's notion of true poetry that his comments on technical linguistic matters and on the role of the poet are so worthwhile. The papers contain many short passages of interest. Here are three:

guessing what goes on in the brain—
When a poet presents a series of logical thoughts in a poem, it is not to express the logic of these thoughts and thus to allow the reader to draw their logical corrollaries in other mnemonics,—rather it is to force the reader through the thinking of those thoughts, since that process of thinking them is an essential part of the experience

which he wishes to recreate in his reader. It does not matter therefore if one logical series is placed alongside another with which it is logically irreconcilable, provided that both series properly belong to the experience in which they are involved. This explains many apparent inconsistencies in the work of major writers—e.g. Adam's thoughts on death in book X of P.L., Wordsworth in Tintern Abbey. (Notebook)

Two problems for poet. (a) which type of poetry within narrative to develop? (b) how to fit this qualified narrative for the expression of modern complexities. Both these answered to some extent by imagism and all best modern narrative poetry has developed from imagism.
(Typewritten lecture notes, assumed to be Singer's)

G. M. Hopkins 'must appear always to participate on one side only in a battle the essence of which is that it is fought *on both sides at every level by all men*. The dogmatic truth, that is, wars with the experiential truth and [. . .] poetic truth is experiential (hence its uselessness in *dogmatic* propaganda) . . . (Notebook)

Singer's view in this last extract is very close to that expressed by Solzhenitsyn in his Nobel Prize address. The political implications of Singer's poetry are not dogmatic but (or should it be 'and'?) they amount to a powerful defence of modes of social and personal existence in which man's capacities are fully extended.

No doubt this is why he wrote so as to lay his poems open to all readers, not just to literary readers. Most difficulties arise from the acuteness of his observation, whether of mental or of physical processes and effects. The reader who is not 'tuned in' to his attitudes may fail to follow the drift. Nevertheless, Singer's own description of how one may meet the truest meanings of poetry cannot be bettered. In the broadcast script 'These Poets and You People' he says:

A poem is an attempt, however indirect, to alter you, to add to you, to give a new value to your life. Only you can judge if it has been successful. If a poem doesn't mean anything to you and you say it is mere blether then you are doing a service to poetry. You may be wrong. That is not the point. You are at least preserving the basic ground of honesty in which it is possible to be right, rather than corrupting your conscience with the pretence of a reverence you do not feel. Through such corruption it is impossible to say or hear anything, least of all a poem.

This selection will, I hope, bring Singer's poetry to the judgement of a wide audience, the audience to which he was himself committed.

ANNE CLUYSENAAR

SHORTER POEMS

A SORT OF LANGUAGE

Who, when night nears, would answer for the patterns
Words will take on? emerging huge, far, shiny,
What unfrequented systems? Or like clouds
Unseen and hiding brightness, bringing rain,
Progressions that the wind drives on, drives after,
Who will say? I who have seen, seen many,
Imagining I scattered them abroad,
Starlight for Calvary and the immense equations
That drew to unity two who knew not either,
As to a hill at midnight, I have seen words,
Seen them with thanks too, shivering, become
Fragile and useless, pale as the steel sparks
Tramcars make waifs of when they round a corner.

STILL AND ALL

I give my word on it. There is no way
Other than this. There is no other way
Of speaking. I am my name. I find my place
Empty without a word, and my word is
Given again. It is nothing less than all
Given away again, and all still truly
Returned on a belief. Believe me now.
There is no other. There is no other way.

These words run vertical in their slim green tunnels
Without any turning away. They turn into
The first flower and speak from a silent bell.
But underneath it is as always still
Truly awakening, slowly and slowly turning
About a shadow scribbled down by sunlight
And turning about my name. I am in my
Survival's hands. I am my shadow's theme.

My shadow's ground feeds me with roots, and rhymes
My statement over. Its radius feeds my flames
Into a cool tunnel. And I who find your ways
About me (In every part I find your ways
Of speech.) pierce ground and shadow still. The light
Is struck. Its definition makes me my quiet
Survival's answer. All still and all so truly
Wakening underneath me and turning slowly.

It's all so truly still. I'll take you into
The first statement. I'll take you along cool tunnels
That channelled light and petalled an iridescent
Symmetry over my bruised shadow. And yes
I'll take you, and your word will follow me,
Till definitions gather distilled honey
And make their mark the fingerprints of light.
I am, believe me then, the name I write.

I lie here still. Yes, truly still. And all
My deliberate identities have fallen

Away with the word given. I find my place
In every place, in every part of speech,
And lie there still. I let my statements go.
A cool green tunnel has stepped in the light of my shadow
There is no way round it. It leads to the flower
Bell—that swings slowly and slowly over.

YOUR WORDS, MY ANSWERS

Then what is it I am
To make of what I mean?
What words will take it down
Through the disputed realm
Where you and I across
An oblique imperative
Meet one another's loss?
Let that fierce statute give
Us new authority
Which takes away our claim
To saying what we mean:
Like the two limbs of a cross
Your words, my answers lie
Together in the place
Where all our meanings die.

POEM WITHOUT A TITLE

It was so fragile a thing that
Suddenly we were afraid of
What would happen if it
Overtook us; and,
Frightened, we ran.

Then came a new fear that
Perplexed us, because we couldn't
Link fear with the beauty which it
Had brought near us, when,
Frightened, we ran.

We now knew only that
It had seemed terrible (but
Not because we might break it,
Rather it us); so,
Frightened, we ran.

Yet still more terrible that,
It being about to vanish,
Our whole lives should depend on it
Utterly. Therefore,
Frightened, we ran.

Later we learned that
Outside we could find nothing
Which would replace it, nor reach it
Within ourselves, though,
Frightened, we ran.

A LETTER

Tonight I'll meet you: yes, tonight. I know
There are, perhaps, a thousand miles—but not
Tonight. Tonight I go inside. I take
All the walls down, the bric-a-brac, the trash,
The tawdry pungent dust these months have gathered
Into a heap about me. I must prepare
And somehow move away from the slow world,
The circling menace with its throat and teeth
Attempting definition; and brush off
Those thoughts that, clinging like thin fallen hairs,
Make me unclean: for I must go tonight
And, secret from my shadow, go alone
Back to the hour when you yourself became
So much my own that even my own eyes
Seemed strange compared to you who were a new
Complete pervasive organ of all sense
Through which I saw and heard and more than touched
The very dignity of experience.

THE LIMITS OF MOVEMENT

I mark my limits on an alighting whirl
          Of wings near daybreak
Birds that are fetched into the sunlight call
          Me by mistake.
I hear the sun that bars my path unfurl
          Songs in my wake.
It keeps me and, in its gallant mood, it will
          Rise for my sake.

We climb down into the street. The smoke
That took my breath away, you took
From such a dot of light. And O,
My dear, as we both turn to go
Back to the herring town where pubs
Await their crews from little ships,
The light and blindness disappear
Together—these songs grow all the more clear.

What a pale text I have put on.
But who is there here who can fathom
This brazen town suddenly quiet
—Not even milk yet laid out?
All else we know to be beyond
Us now. Confined here we both wonder
Whether, like these stones, we must also
Be quarried, built with, before we can grow.

Roll up. Roll up. See the stage-cut stars on the streets
Every performance is a first-night showing.
Every entrance the last—and there are no exits.

LIE DISTANT, MY GOOD LIGHT

Lie distant, my good light,
Parted from part of me.
Yet distantly delight
With instaneity.

This rain will not abate.
Winds knock at the wall.
Good light, reintegrate
The silence of us all.

VERSES FROM A DISTANCE

Gently, my darling, I will hurt by saying
But the one word that it would hurt to silence.
I smother it in every syntax, miming
With different motions but a constant meaning
Till strangers marvel at my way of living.

They see a hurry that is hardly living;
They hear me babble yet I am not saying
Any word, am simply breaking silence,
Silence that seeps out through my heart's miming,
My heart that's breaking with its sense of meaning.

A sense significant but hardly meaning,
More than the wind because it moves is living,
Or than the sea because it sounds is saying,
For my whole heart is breaking into silence
And its disruption is a kind of miming.

Concordant movement that is hardly miming
Of pieces that were blasted with their meaning
Into a new and anxious way of living
Becomes the content of what I am saying
In a vocabulary made of silence.

Soundless intelligence that is hardly silence
Goes out from me through this disordered miming,
Out to my darling who will know the meaning
Of the calamity that we are living
Who cannot speak what our two lives are saying.

A hope, a prayer perhaps, but hardly saying,
Since the whole syntax of our love is silence
And all love's motions are in us made miming:
Maimed and unable is our love's true meaning:
Only the sorrow in us is left living.

A LANDSCAPED ROOM

Now that these threats
Like grey hairs
Hedge the sun's
Chubby brilliance,
Its boy's brash face
Discountenanced
By clouds and rains,
Two panes of glass
Shortsightedly
Glaze roughened stones,
The garden soil's
Moist breathing
Gathered outside.

'Keep distance out',
The carpet cries.
A door dreams.
Walls sulk.
Warmth whispers
Threatened by mirrors.

But a discord
From overhead
Tumbles, trickles
And blackens the garden.
The greyhaired sun
Hears, as golden
Boys never can,
The patter of tears
In the deep distance.

An adult sun
Listens to trouble.
No answer is given.
The question rests.

The door crumples.
The carpet cries.
Stones return
The unbroken look
And distance sneers
At the room's two
Hollow eyes.

THE MOTH

The light browses, wading these shallow walls
As though it could be patient, but can not.
The light comes through and gradually recalls
Me to a place that no-one would have thought
Hidden within the manoeuvring waterfalls,
The trim cascades. The walls. The walls. The walls.

A death's head moth is fluttering in my room.

Darkness knocks at the window. I hear it move.
The light is trying to reach it but can not.
Land is outside, earth and the fields I love
And would be still as, but that every thought
Makes flesh a wall of water where lights have
Drunk and gone on. They move. They move. They move.

A death's head moth is fluttering in my room.

I follow hard on a whole herd of light,
And try to see by it, but I can not.
Only the walls, water, land, windows, darkness, night,
Impel themselves at me. My flesh and thought
Feel for a destination, but my sight
Meets only light. The light. The light. The light.

A death's head moth is fluttering in my room.

THE PRESENT

This is a place that wounds,
Then falls apart,
Maimed out of symmetry
Like my own heart.

I come down here to gather
Recollections:
Stained, counterstained, my tissues
In micron sections.

I gather information
On the extent
Of loss, of profit lost,
—And pay my rent.

I live here though the place
Is stiff, restricted:
It bandages the wounds
Its walls inflicted.

SUNLIGHT

It was a dream in night,
The pier all ropes, a road,
Houses, tiles a-tilting,
Where only sunlight stood.

My bus was made of bridges,
Words I had overheard,
Small streets and talking cages,
Shells that secreted a bird.

It was the South of France.
I climbed the high-built bus
In a sparse but limitless landscape
I knew I could not pass.

So I reversed the corner.
I did not turn. I jumped.
And down on me hard and heavy
Mountains of sunlight were dumped,

With an English pub in the centre
Where wines were cold and dry
And I could feel the sunlight's
Smooth intensity.

Therefore farewell, my lovely;
It was towards you I went
When into dreams at midnight
Summer sunlight bent.

A SMALL GRIEF HAS BEEN LAUNCHED

These headlands clench their bare grey talons
Deep into the splash of water, and they scrape
Whitenesses out of waves caught half off-balance
By the burly steadiness of this gaunt cape.

And further out, invisibly exiled there,
Where the full swim of the sea floats salt shoals
Over its bows, under its keel, there rolls
That one small grief, that broken part of prayer.

Of course unseen, naturally, because
The scream of rocks scraping the edge is me.
I am deserted for those anonymous
Regularities of the implacable sea.

Though I can't follow it, though I must
Grasp scant purity from the shallows; although
These stones, my selves, this humid solid dust
That baulks the ocean determines all I know.

There is the grief in exile; somewhere, it
Divides distance, punctuates freedom, soars.
I stand and grasp at water, squat, spit,
Myself my anchor since my selves are shores.

But still the grief, no longer mine, makes free
With every weather and sails on out,
Safe agent, slackened by no rusting doubt
Since it obeys each inch of each decree.

Bound to that wave, it bounds away to this:
Missing, it topples: toppling, is rescued by
The waters of its previous jeopardy:
Directions take it now, a dot of distance.

A dot of distance keeping to its course
Away from me, it rides those changing laws,

This little grief, once mine, now lost in hoarse
Commands that carry it: and yet it draws

The best of me and what I hope to learn
Out into depths these talons cannot reach
And over depths unknown to any speech
Towards shores that dwarf my blind but best concern.

PARTING

Let me forget that I may forgive you
The enmity of this silence,
The necessity of this comfort,
The lingering of this anguish,
My incapacity to love you.

Let me forget, for I have pretended
Comprehension of what
I could not hope to reach,
Could not possess, could not
Leave and love uncomprehended.

Pretended love, pretended
Fear and passion, all,
Now all is almost ended
But forgiving and forgetting,
That is everywhere extended.

I TELL YOU STRAIGHT

I tell you straight the memory is
Either the best or worst of this,

The most intense, the least like what
Life seems to be and yet is not:

But most intense this memory is
Like life that lingers on to kiss

The shadows underneath the skin
Which that lamp cast, unlit for sin.

PETERHEAD IN MAY

Small lights pirouette
Among these brisk little boats.
A beam, cool as a butler,
Steps from the lighthouse.

Wheelroom windows are dark.
Reflections of light quickly
Skip over them tipsily like
A girl in silk.

One knows there is new paint
And somehow an intense
Suggestion of ornament
Comes into mind.

Imagine elephants here.
They'd settle, clumsily sure
Of themselves and of us and of four
Square meals and of water.

Then you will have it. This
Though a grey and quiet place
Finds nothing much amiss.
It keeps its stillness.

There is no wind. A thin
Mist fumbles above it and,
Doing its best to be gone,
Obscures the position.

This place is quiet or,
Better, impersonal. There
Now you have it. No verdict
Is asked for, no answer.

Yet nets will lie all morning,
Limp like stage scenery,
Unused but significant
Of something to come.

BIRDSONG

The speck of protoplasm in a finch's egg,
—Watch it under its spotted shell—
It will one day be pinned upon a treetop
To curl the tresses of the straight blond breeze
With auburn musics, auspicious sunburnt notes
That are for me the triumph of the scenery.

Already, quietly, it winds temptations,
Harnesses the young blood
And bridles it with promises of discovery
To the delights which all the old ones know
Are, in success, as pointless as the breeze
Or these sharp spangles trammelling the wind's beak.

HOW THEN DID WE EVER ARRIVE

How then did we ever arrive
(In the house with the hill under it, under us held
Together by staples and stones, cemented; nailed
Against one another, and driven against one another) arrive
Alone in the open sea?
The humped back of a whale, salt bodies we drive
In a hot spurt out of us into insensitive
Air where they stagger like ninepins together, while separate
     we
Sink back into the wave.
It drives over us, drives us on under it down.
Then swims slowly, sleepwalking the ocean, to drown
In its own white hair: and drowns us and leaves us with
     nothing to save
But bodies built in wet skin.
I do not know whether all this can deprive
Us of dry land, a house, the stubble, where love
Moves like a farmer and staggers and knows his parks to the
     bone
And lets harvest arrive.

WIFE

> *She, she herself, and only she*
> *Shone through her body visibly.*
> —Coleridge

Your dark body deepens suddenly.
Over the meagre firth where children throw
Pennies for luck or where the drowned imago
Is eaten by orphaned infants, about as high
As the horizon's level in the eye,
An eager trapdoor swings upon a screw.
Already, as the door gives under you,
Its prodigies, secretly seen, uncover the lie
Of your deepening understanding, your
Motion towards palpable invisibility.
As usual, when things matter, some of us die.
I drown in what I am, among the obscure
Instants that cannot teach me to endure
Your dark body deepening gradually.

TO MARIE

For Half a Year of Happiness
November 6th: 1956

For half a year of happiness
    Between us two
These small barefooted words must run
    Along my pen to you.

They whisper secretly in one
    Another's secret ear:
Heavy black-booted thoughts patrol,
    But cannot hear.

This mob of children from the streets
    Where love is young and we
Playing pavement games, chalk clumsy signs
    And riddle-ree.

O do not be deceived, my dear.
    Sing me a song.
These little gangs, in secret gay,
    Have beaten down those long

Vocabularies, squads of words,
    In sulky navy-blue.
There's half a year of happiness
    Between us two.

GOODNIGHT

Lie on my left side, darling. It is time
For us to sleep now. Underneath us tumble
Keen little eyes like pincers which take aim
At the sad centre these delights preamble.
No, yesterday will never be the future
Nor will tonight; but afterwards, who knows
In what fine body I'll foresee a feature
Of her through whom my true love undergoes?

Across the vase where last week's flowers look up
Decay is complex in them; they impend
Backwards to watch you: we try to understand
How you will melt my darling, but we slip
Underneath, stagnant: or, simplified beyond
The simplification of shadows, fall asleep.

AN APOLOGY

It is the unforgivable
Essence of individual acts
Which uncontrollably attracts
Words through the incommunicable.

It is the story of a sin
Committed against our every dream
Of what we might one day become
Outwardly as we were within.

It is the story of a graph
Aimed at a bare infinity
But keeping in its inky way
Steadily to its paper path.

It is the story of a man
Who travelled far but could not find
One person whom he did not wound:
Until, deserted, he began

Making his shadow into bone
And on that bone put flesh of light
Which shone back with a passionate
Will to forgive him and atone.

WORDS MADE OF WATER

Men meet and part;
But meeting men today
I find them frightened,
Frightened and insolent,
Distrustful as myself.
We turn arrogantly toward one another,
Caged in dogmatical dazzle.
Our eyes shine like thin torchlight.
Conflicting truths, we dazzle one another.
Never lately have I known men meet
With only darkness, quite anonymous,
Perched up between them on a song no bird
Would answer for in sunlight.
I have watched carefully but never once
Have I seen the little heaps,
The co-ordinated fragments of muscle, brain, bone,
Creep steadfastly as ants across the planet,
Quite lost in their own excess of contraries,
Make signals, ask for answers,
Humbly and heavily from those they know
Are equally ignorant.

Looking about the streets I find the answers,
Thin blobs of light, enamelled price-lists, brawling,
An impatient competition
Between all those who all know all the answers.

I find also certain bits of paper,
Matchsticks, sodden or cracked or still with safety heads,
Cigarette douts and their empty packets,
And also water,
Water that is stagnant
Or water flowing slowly down the gutter.

I sometimes think that dead men live in water,
That their ghosts inhabit the stagnant puddles,
Their barges float with the gutter water
That they are waiting patiently as water

Until the world is redeemed by doubt,
By each man's love for all those different answers
Dead men have dropped on sundry bits of paper,
From glances blue as smoke, now quite extinguished.

My womenfolk find these thoughts troubling.
Action becomes impossible: choice is impossible
To those who think such things.
On thoughts like these no man ever grew fat.

THE MEN OF NOW

Yet one more day more level in deceit
And the long green-springing furrows that plot in my brow
Winding over prehistory over the street
In an uneven and half-hidden grandeur:
A sheet of sheaves, they corpse more handsome a harvest
Than falls our lot among the men of now.

Yet one day more more loyal to deceit
My Judas springtime hears the streetline echo
With the kiss of my journey that hurries, afraid to be late,
Afraid of the plunge of the mine, of the sob of the well,
That deep underfoot might erupt, bury or veil
In ascending deluge; collapsing, might squander and wreck.

Yet one day more and never nearer death
I wait and write. Remember this at least:
That one man running home was out of breath
For fear of the mines and the veins aligned in the earth,
Their undiscovered riches waiting for birth:
Remember this, and try to be appeased.

THE TRUE COMPANY

From that beginning which alters toward
Total stability and toward
Every beginning's alteration
Through its decaying assignation
The true company keeps its word.

Semantics now, being at least
As modern as old, it yet brings past
Us, as it passes, ancient weapons
To show us that whatever happens
Happened also to gods and a ghost.

The gods, grown weary with literal
Divinity, sneered, and, sneering, they fell
Into sin to find new versions
Of innocence. Godly abortions
Unborn, unsinning, took them to Hell.

Literally too, the ghost could
Frighten children and haunt a wood.
But now the only ghost is dying
Of believing in the lying
Claim it had made it never should.

Swords sweat and swagger as the true
Company continues through
Each alteration in superstition
And hacks it down to belief. Transition
Cannot alter what it can do.

Its word is kept, throughout the absurd
Systems religions it rushes toward,
Clean, meaningful, sacerdotal.
Through all changes it keeps the total
Stability of the exact word.

THE BEST OF IT

The best of it is that I am at least
Made less by what is greater, and that I can't,
Reached by these words now, measure what's increased.

Your words make hay of me, but I'm released
By them from standing shivering and distant.
The best of it is that I am at least.

Knees soaked rheumatic by the promised harvest
You razed with scythe and sickle what I meant:
Reached by these words now, measure what's increased.

But you, like a horizon or a priest,
Past every boundary of the round land, went:
The best of it is that I am at least
Reached by these words now measuring what's increased.

S. O. S. LIFESCENE

That plunging mast, nailed to a whirligig gale,
Shows its three sheer signs of drowning. Those crewed wet
        boards
Drag at the spray. Oceans drip backwards and forth
From that tall steel prow, those seamen, crouched that sail.

Crouched to climb: cling of the white wetnesses,
Heave of the sea's deep sheets, wheezing like twenty
Conferences stacked round tables, pressing
Processions, quarrel of kingdoms: pitch salt centre.

Out of it, down from it, hangs the electric shout,
Nine gooseflesh sparks breathing white out on the rabble
Of sweaty and swaggering gales. Held hard to the squabbling
Waters, to Save Our Souls the sounds fade out.

Yet steered, here steered, and over the sea's salt dregs
Set climbing forth, is crewed by the conscious and steered,
Wheeled in two knotted hands through the callous but prayer-
Breasting, heart-wresting hour, is ruddered with rags.

For the men, backed out to the bone, catch up on the past
In a straight line, like winter . . . the trees. Burn back
The barren courses, confront the naked mistake,
The embezzled hours accounted, the fake blot erased.

Talk yourself out of it! Out of it! Talk yourself! Talk!
And a death's click closes those offices foaming with grins.
That stoke-black lascar, damp and salt with work,
Looks through a lurch at the red wreck under his skin.

That engineer who's thistle-eyed for sleep
Circles the clock through goaded hoops and trances
To where she departs . . . to where she hurries . . . she dances . . .
The damp cellar and whisky . . . the heart in a heap . . .

S.O.S. it repeats, repeats, told, retold.
Small white far cry for help as they kindle close

Together or blaze in a curse. For the storm grows
To death for the captain and the boy blown blue by the cold.

Corked nets and clinging baits, those sodden boards
Muscled about by their men, drag deep at the shoals
And their hooked catchings draw blood. But bite to the core!
There are nine white pips crying 'help' in a black bowl.

Seeds of the storm, quick fish, the intense alone
Of their human cry, where the storm bleats down like a ram
And the waves whinny away; where the smooth sky's brown
Blacks out, and the stars are dead and don't matter a damn.

What matters is the cry, the cry like a screw,
Sharp-oiled to turning, clean-cutting fish-silver through
And through the teak air,
A makeshift repetitive batter to rivetting prayer.

Like stitching sails this windfall patches men,
Question to answer, push and heave and tug,
Thick-fibred needlework, an electric plug,
Nine cock-crows savage the air and cry us all home.

HOME FROM THE SEA

The longest days are those spent at sea.
Waves dip heavily, trundling under our gunwale
An imagination or promise of the ocean as abyss.
The longest days are those we can hardly remember.
Dead waters retire. The smoke lingers unshaven
Or lounges from cabins into a corridor where
It collides helplessly with the stink of coffee.

There is no steadiness anywhere except in the arrival
Of another wave or another morning. The same
Unsteadiness, waves morning by morning,
Jolts without jest our neurotic banter.

Slowly around us the air circulates like
A paper that everyone has already re-read
And will re-read later. Ghostly
The engines clamber through the floor.

Cards collect grease from many fingers. Dust
Rubs along the ward-room to the galley.
The great sea collapses harmlessly outside
An unopening door.

Slipshod and sleepy, we calculate who we are.

We sit beside the clock that thuds so softly
Around in circles and dictates our duties.
Its monosyllables never threaten us.
We know we're safe; since, though the ocean flexes
Its watery muscles with a vast display,
There is inside those ships which sail the farthest
A shabby but invulnerable place that hedges
Stability with repetitive concision.

The clock, in monosyllables, repeats,
Time out of mind and out of time with ours,
A mile, a mile, another mile, until
One day it stops, neglected, unwound,
The current turned off: this is our destination.

CORNER BOY'S FAREWELL

In the yellow room among the grey furniture I sit sorrowfully
Already sour with the wisdom of age and bitterly complaining.
Outside the evening sulks away.
The garden vegetation curls up like a cat.
The hillside tumbles a snug green wall.
Why do they keep coming back, the days we have spent
      together?
They come in their long lines but dancing and deep in the sun,
Deep in the sun, black and engraved in shadows.
Why do they keep coming back with such regular purpose?

First in the club-room,
The grumbling inconsequent people
Arguing art over stale tea-bread . . .
And I very young was greatly impressed.
You hardly saw me through their foggy heads.
Bluebottles clung to the damp flycatcher. My eyes were glued
      on your face.
You hardly saw me. Then you went away.

Between parting and our second meeting
Months passed and many things happened.
During that time my heart and mind were hid.
The twins of the wood were hid from woodcutters'
Eyes, from the temptations of the house of sugar.
I hid them alive in the shape of a drunken bout.
I put them to sleep in the dugs of a dried-up whore.
I silvered round in tinfoil cartons, talked them into the noisy
      drugs,
To hide from my grand accusers, from the huge scenery of
      your great disciples.
And yet when we finally met again,
You, half mad with your own problems:
I, an absconded schoolboy:
Our laughter was green in the London pubs
And a sympathy somehow occurred that was not to be
      laughed at.

And after that time the occasions of meeting gather:
From the ends of this country, from the cramped edges of
    experience
They trek in a single direction that makes us separate ever.
I cannot quite remember all the dates and places
But we have stood at corners, sat together
Between apprisal and dismissal,
Arrival and departure,
Between anticipation and delight,
Boisterous days and the long memory.
We have stood at corners and waited together.
What I remember best is saying goodbye
For that is most in the nature of friendship.

A week ago in this selfsame city
We said farewell and did not know we said it.
And I was left to revile in this rainy place.
O my poems, be against this city:
Its people badly dressed and without good manners,
The simplest necessities of life made lewd and tortuous.
Let them be things of a day.
Let my poems have bees' blood in them,
Let them be sharp but sensitive to honey.
For I still think of life as once of mist in Cornwall
Man-high and from the sea subsiding gently
Over the ploughed fields, brown, with scarce green growth,
But hidden under field-grey all that day,
Woven to one opacity.
Then on my eyesight the slant light broke
Of a single mist-drop narrowly slung to a cobweb
And each, the mist, through which my senses travelled
Broke at that sun-reflecting signal to its own:
The watered air grew bright with single claws:
So on the fine web spun from something stronger
One man can hold, precarious, complete
His own self's light that never is repeated
But acts as orrery to all the lights of others:
And that same web grows finer with its function,
More beautiful to praise with each drop held
In that peculiar tension once forever.

That's how I think of you and your calm discourse,
And thinking too the knowledge of a minute,
Planet's discovery or the seed of tree,
A new tree in a new place, something
To come, to grow gradually actual,
Thinking of this and that and all together
You grow so bright I sometimes seem to see
Walking between you and the direct sun
My evening-shadow struggling like a breeze
Until it climbs against it, smothers light
And drowns the sun out down beneath your face.

For that is the special human knowledge,
Knowledge of genesis
Of a brightness other than that of the day sun,
Outstaring and outstripping.
And this is human too
—Though valid more than for humanity,
Humanity its instrument—this knowledge
That I have hit on since you went
Of going further out than light can follow, rooted and
        separate,
Into America, my mind or sea.
This I prepare for and communicate
In the anticipation of my lifelong voyage
Of seeing what has always been most loved grow dim and
        disappear
Into perfection's prodigies of peace.

Into the sacrifice bitterly endless of all that man means
In terms of bones, breath, skin and brain,
Of his achievements, even the love humility achieved.
Love he can only like a beggar take
From the kind hand of passage hidden in his heart,
The hand that could be merciless as he,
Deny as he denies.

Love he is given, he who, like a beggar,
Squats where the virtues congregate their outpour,
He who is hasty when a dime of knowledge

Drops in his cap
To run and spend it in the nearest brothel
And then come howling back to the mercy and lucky down-
    pouring.
This knowledge then of leaving all behind
All, that by wailing meanly, may attend my vigil.

FOR JOSEF HERMAN

Nothing, nothing, nothing
Can never ever happen
To this man who sits here
Some distance from the river.

His plump and portly hands
Conjure the daylight out
Of the pits' blackness and
Absorb the sun of Spain.

The Hebrides are his,
The ghetto and the city.
His loneliness is such
That children love to share it.

Companionship is his
And wise frivolities.
I wonder, if you could look
Quietly into his eyes

And they laughed as confidently
As the humming wings of flies,
If it would seem to you
That you had never died.

SONNETS FOR A DYING MAN

I.

To talk to you in all moralities,
Each to its true end mastered, till all one
Their intertwining helpful verities
Collapse across the gesture of your pain,
And then begin, replete in my whole tongue,
Each blind persuasion searched and hidden in
Its language luminously, at last begin
To tell you that, impossibly as you clung
To what you could not keep, what clings to you
Claws at its own ghost also yet to be
Created by your death, that though it try
To filch the pain which you are living through
It cannot take it: nothing can undo
The immortality of the day you die.

II.

My children, come. Read in this book at bed-
Time of the times you cannot, and my dear
Procession through the uprisen words I've said
Hear of the fall at springtime from the year.
Loud though it buds, exactly to a head,
Springtime is time to hush and overhear
Perpetual ambush, treading on the dead
Spit of another springtime, disappear.
For to that fall it is I'll alter your
Words from the words uprising through my mouth
Unripened in procession: they'll fall for sure
When, and exactly then, they've said their truth.
Words of my mouth and children of my name
Come down from springtime, for the springtime came.

III.

Break words with me: what little silence may
Still live in minds and minds communicate
That will I give you, or at any rate
The palpable image of what I cannot say.
Break silence with me: let the interplay
Of breath and breathing agonies relate
Another quietness to a better state
Than this slow parting will allow today.
At this breath taking let us both believe
What we have disbelieved, but not because
Of any terror or of any laws.
Let us break up all words that do not grieve.
But let us keep the truth, the truth that keeps
Us both alive when either of us sleeps.

IV.

Not more than quietly that a loud land
Take back its thunder from a threatened sky
And you by heartfelt rigour understand
Why the grave dust should not be asking: Why?
But actual quiet yet, and a clear command
To wheesht away and hush each wild reply,
The eye that angered at the sight of sand,
The bones that hollered: Mud can never die.
Thus to accept: yes, quietly to have found
Life at the end of life by dying as
The least of things and least preposterous
Of the infinities that robe you round,
Not more than quietly let your loud lives lie
Down in the grave that overhangs the sky.

V.

These words outdistance us. Voices run down
On slates that echo with the things we said
And splash new blood till chimneys streaming red
Beacon the traffic from another town.
The sun is in them and the damp clouds frown
Fertile from out of them upon a head
That, though it lives, can understand the dead
Who whisper in the sea and do not drown.
Not mine alone but many lives have brought
These words to life and live again as I
Search to return them to the simple thought
That will extravagantly multiply
Your life through death and ravel up the knot
That binds their utterance to eternity.

VI.

Because it's here (out there arrivals spin
Identities beyond us) and it's now we feel
Throngs thudding out of water to begin
Quietness in us and we find them real,
Because it's here at last, and because we can't
Draw a breath nearer now it's reached us and
It comes here searching us, is off the scent
Of what in all ourselves we understand,
We're more alive for it, for learning how
It's come that long way from us to fetch down
Familiar vengeance, and it lets us know,
As best we can, what never can be known
And can't be seen until, now that it's here,
We watch it reach us as we disappear.

VII.

This place has come to you. It's lost your way
And now, man-eating on their nightly scout,
Contours instead of colours set you out
Upon a map that bumps up to betray
Your stillness to you as you stand at bay
And hear the wilderness (or did you shout?)
Howl for a road to light it towards your doubt
Which it will have devoured before the day.
It creeps diminishing within you till
It is yourself and you, an open door,
Flap in the wind at nothing: sea and sky
Have disappeared within the earth you fill
Who now learn what you may have guessed before
You do not know the world in which you die.

VIII.

From all your worlds with all their repetition
To the discovery when they stopped and fell,
Love was the unconditional condition
Of peace in heaven or of hope in hell.
This world has worlds which are its worlds apart
Where centuries prolong a summer fable
Into that inmost miracle of the heart,
The love whose listening is irrevocable.
From all your deaths all songs are lullabies
To the awakening when all deaths have gone
Down into darkness and the dark worlds dawn.
From all your deaths love floats its worlds, and cries
To you to follow by the million on
A fugue of footsteps of immense replies.

IX.

Come into exile, prisoner, from the vault
Where memories draw your blood and the blood dissolves
Your features. Used as a butt, your every fault
Made critical hostage by your congested selves,
You, like a rascal's puppet, dangle on
Spurs, snakes, and fire. Cut into ghosts, your flesh
Inflamed, burnt hollow, your very mind is drawn
Apart, its thoughts taught tortures, turned to trash.
And yet if once Prince Exile call you home,
Your hopes his mild disciples, but your cage
Miraculously otherwise and rare,
Your rascal selves rally, and you become
Precious to them, and they revolting rage
Down hours and arteries to defend despair.

X.

I close your door behind me carefully
And walk into myself upon your bed
In the thick street where the remaining sky
Skims the horizon from a chimney's head.
Rocks stuck together build up to a dome.
Snow scuffles off the main road under wheels.
You melt out bloodlessly and become the home
Of my own being till my blood congeals.
Men go inside the stones and disappear.
The roofs are white-washed, turning brown, like snow,
And as that goes this city too must go.
There is another roof beneath us here
In the man-eating landscape in your room
Which I will not leave till I reach the tomb.

XI.

Your voice turns in me like a talking knife:
Your blood rusts mine: your bones have turned to teeth:
Your lungs inhale the remnants of my life:
And I am murdered by your whispered faith.
And yet I live, and you are still betrayed.
I'm more than anything that man in me
Who would forget you and who has arrayed
My selves against their own infinity.
Your enemy within me takes his turn
At talking. I am that man he'd gladly burn
And he is my accuser. You two meet
And with one voice you both accuse me: yet
You each know that as every hour was born
I stole my life to lay it at your feet.

XII.

Keening away in quietness as best
I, the intruder, can, at your last hour,
When, being lost, you, by discovery blest,
Like an old pirate finding a new shore,
Lag, though outdistancing all that went before,
Upon a land beyond what you had guessed,
Within the body that will find your rest,
Far, far, behind the person that you are,
I recognize the stranger: I reply
Across the ghost at his occasional
Polite beck of the hand: I give you all
The things we give the dying: and then I,
Smoothing your sheets as quietly as I may,
Find that I've said the things I cannot say.

XIII.

You who crop up between the world and me,
You the king gooseberry with the ace of spades
Who ride in silent riot as in raids,
If sores were weapons, Vikings rode the sea:
You with the snoop-looks, here to disagree,
Or spoil the whisky, sap the lemonade,
Or to dissect the corpse from an old maid
Who wobbles outdoors on a spending spree:
You who when most I want to be alone
Come interloping with one bottle more
Of bitter stuff that turns the blood to bone
And makes dust burn where muscles bulged before:
You who are dying of the life I live
If you can read these verses then forgive.

XIV.

For all its rich bravado there's the skull,
Big bones and little, thick thin flat curly ones,
Fastened together in a poor white ball:
And underneath it lies the skeleton's
Facsimile of a man. Though the man can't
Cry any longer or deny the truth
This represents him, and for all its scant
Structural pieties he is this beneath.
The baffled mother scrapes her little son
Into a vase. The battlefield looks land
Until you notice blistered corpses in
Ditches, at back of dykes, half under sand.
The son looks up to see his mother frown
And caterpillars crawling through the skin.

XV.

The old man dozed. The hospital quietened.
Nurses went whispering past his unmade bed:
While Mr Childs, who has no stomach, yawned
And those with papers put them by, unread.
It went all right till tea-time. Then the trays
Trickling like iron water through the ward
Wakened the old man and in prompt relays
The nurses gathered to be reassured.
The old man wakened but to what old tales
Of overwork or underpay or hate
We'll never know. By now it is too late.
But Mr Childs, who has no stomach, swore
The old man rose and tried to shout before
His eyes went slimy with the look of snails.

XVI.

This, I suppose, is what they mean by death,
The senses clogged, the air inhaled upon us:
Your chest is snatched at, torn by your own breath,
While doctors search you for exotic faunas.
Fix the glass slide in flame, stain, and remark
That chain of streptococci under oil.
You look up like a dog that wants to bark
While they transmit your heartbeat through a coil.
Merciful monster, doctor with a serum,
Look at your own eyes in my instrument
And then correct your inferential theorem
About what death is, or rather what you meant.
All you intended was, of course, no lie:
Admit it though, you didn't *mean* to die.

XVII.

The things our ignorance tries to reconcile
With a bright good imagined in the summer
As something of a spiritual tremor
Or in the winter as an icicle,
Remain in contradiction all the while:
For though there is the dream there is the dreamer
Who seeks and sucks from them his every humour,
Nor was the world invented by his smile.
It is hard fact and fertile with its proofs
Of what is possible within it and
Impossible for us to understand.
It is a rabble of self-evident truths
With no invention added, no demand
For a new meaning from the one at hand.

XVIII.

Shadows are fruit let fall by the cramped sun:
Its permanent orbit, blazing pedestal,
Contracted by criss-crossing to a cell
In which we watch it prowling while we run.
We run to reach new systems which have none
Of its or our spry littleness. We call
Our lives out after us. They swell, dispel
The place they were alive in, and are gone.
That, of course suicide, is how we live.
In our immensities we disappear.
As if they'd struck and been quenched in a tear
Planets burn black to us which cannot give
More light than that we knew when from the sun
Ripe shadows rained hard on us as we fell.

XIX.

Even as at first, when every world loomed damned
Over us, hang over, avalanche ready to fall,
There came Christ, and the Buddha came, and they calmed
Those they led inwards to a still higher hill,
So doubt redeemed us. When our experience
Made nonsense of itself and let us think
Each thought mere thought, it gave us a defence
Against the unthinkable, a blot on invisible ink.
The process was—we knew we could not know—
Different from knowledge. The world was our surprise
And when it came to peer into our eyes
We thought that we were learning, and we learned slow.
We learned too late. God, like an iceberg, was
Already neck-deep in our godless laws.

XX.
The certainty in the forest wears a green colour:
Blue wisdoms rise from water: and the sky knows
Principles penetrating tall rainbows:
Man learns by doubt: his certainties are hollow.
The seasons also understand one another:
They keep to precedence and, though they alter, no
Quirk in the weather alters how they go:
If man finds means he makes his brothers follow.
Man's moral exactitudes never iron out.
Brainy vitality splits him open to thought:
Then skulls creep out like beetles and turn white.
His red blood's all the metaphor he has
Ever for certainty, and that he must lose
Whenever it is certain that it was.

XXI.

High tiding anchors us. This world is never
So well away aboveboard that it lifts
Us beyond topmost and the dark spills over:
A talisman will hold us lest it drifts.
High heaven banks down at us. We shoal whenever
Its peaceful progress takes us with its gifts
Or heave up steadily till its ocean shifts
Our names for sure upon a solid river.
Not then away, skull. Hug the grave's earth, bone.
World wounds are bandaged by an unwinding sun.
Lie safe beyond all notion that your size
Mimics these infantile infinities.
Let me who have been doing and have done
Lie down beneath a low wall hung with cries.

XXII.

Who the dead are or how to learn their habits
Remain not questions but mere nonsense spelt
Carefully out to us by the way we felt
When we first learned that we must die like rabbits.
Dreams changed to nightmare: now the mind exhibits
Reason perhaps, more likely panic, and
Corruption by an inchtape into titbits
Is all that it pretends to understand.
Its dead are joined by slipknots through the bone:
The pink lank worms have tied them idly fast,
Just as the reasonable live men guessed:
And if a world escapes it's quite unknown,
Since what has perished, having perished, is
Not matter subject to analysis.

XXIII.

Is it perhaps a telephone unanswered,
A sun in trouble, or a star on heat,
The B.B.C. truncating bits of Hansard,
Or is a ghost howling beneath the street?
I do not know what it can be you hear.
I know that you are listening, and I try,
By listening also, not to interfere
With your supreme unshared perplexity.
What words can say to me the words have said
Out there where nothing happens since you are
No longer there for things to happen to
And there's no way of telling what is true
You cannot find me any image for
Our knowledge of our ignorance of the dead.

XXIV.

Weigh anchor into windfall and lurch at last
Up the ribbed ocean, green swell and unruly foam
Combed back in curls beneath you as you climb
On keels in wool and what you're drenched in dressed.
Its purl or plain, its odd or even twist,
Takes your blood nevertheless away towards home
From a heart weighed up more heavy against its doom
Than ever that sailor in a hornpipe lost.
It's worlds away now that the heart's cable croaks
Down to its hold in coils, and it's underneath
The weighed-up world that you with grinning teeth
(Rib-bones for jersey, silence for your jokes)
Will plunge however wind falls, odd or even,
While priests puff prayers to blow your corpse to heaven.

XXV.

What man will speak it all? What man is dead
In his completeness and with not a part
Of this stark world forgotten, but fit to start
An argument with the almighty figurehead?
Proudly his own, he might give God his body:
But his intelligence would, by trim statistics
In the emergency, be always ready
For any trickery in God's linguistics.
Who would let sheep judge shepherds? Who would say
Let only convicts sentence criminals?
Or the insane alone treat sanity?
Yet to what court is it that man appeals?
God—the good criminal, the mad lamb,
Who drowns all protests with the words—'I am.'

XXVI.

This emphasis is older than creation:
That of the uncreate the most valued part
Tugs innocently onward till it start
Solidity from zero's desolation.
The earth pours flowers up that were nowhere sown;
Traditions peel away; and thoughts run free
From something earlier than their memory:
Absurd of course, but things become unknown.
Then the mind alters us, till in the end
Even a past foolishness can somehow amend
Retrospect into prospect: and when we die
We suffer intellectual agony
Foreseeing centuries in which to spend
The time we wept in yet have no tears to dry.

XXVII.

Memory moves against from opposites
Attacking where we are; or it undoes us
Gingerly, by remembering what we lose as
The vectors of ourselves; and nothing fits
Safely without it, and nothing is beyond
Its reach to change, yet nothing alters it
Except by a diminishing from the complete
Past, the imperfect burial, the open ground.
Thus when we watch it as we watch today
Our eyes, employing shadows, see the sun
Dawn out in China, but we can't say when,
Since all occasions enter, all lights play
Their part in ceremonies we have never seen
And strangers dance explaining who we've been.

XXVIII.

Time's acres kindled in the sort of way
That could not burn us back to what we grew
Into at once and always every day
Reached or remained or merely thought we knew.
And having done it what was almost burnt
Flamed and was burnt again, and we were taught
That what we thought was almost what we thought
Was a mere cinder or a phrase recurrent.
But what was burnt, that had gone black indeed.
So time took time to make our legions risk
Their own dark enemy, and the tinkling reed
Which says forever that the winds are brisk
Blew time out windily across our way.
Thus we were ambushed into what we say.

XXIX.

All men and the majestic animals go down,
And worms die too, and the sea monsters die,
And girls and giggling children, king and clown,
All the old platitudes put on a dignity.
But we forget them in the impatient things
They fetch to memory, what they thought was true,
What words replied through questions: and death brings
Oblivion to the particular things they knew.
We can remember them but we know it's not
Them we remember, rather an artifact
In the convenient language of our thought
Pretends it can return them what they lacked,
A place in us, a world beyond memory,
A tenderness that loves anonymously.

XXX.

To see the petrel cropping in the farmyard
Among brown hens, trying in vain to cluck,
Trying to rouse the rooster, trying too hard,
And cursing its enormous lack of luck,
That, or to watch it stalling over snow
Starved, as at last, its energies pegged out,
It fluttering perishes, and it does not know
What water this is though it cannot doubt,
That is not all enough. Remember then
The black bird, white bird, waltzing, gale and all
Fetch, lunge, soar, paddle, with an Atlantic squall
Or semi-Arctic blizzard, until an
Immense sea breaks you and the gunwales grip
And one storm petrel rises like a whip.

XXXI.

Burnt to a life instead and shaped in flame
Messages over the sea and waved up high
As signal soul and flashing soul of the same
Wave-drowning wave, a gashed and glistening ship,
You bend back waters under in a heap
And step above as steep as any dream
The unleashed magnitudes to a sunburnt calm
Waved up and borne within your blazing shape.
Burnt to a life the sea your hull shapes out
Of waves, waves hustle and sizzling waves and that
Tall breaker with a legend in its beak
Come snatching at you into the plunging seawrack,
Swims off beyond the perished and beyond
Swirling horizons and is never found.

XXXII.

Call it by what you will it, but do not
Forget that for the first last time you are
Outdistanced by your hankering metaphor,
Ambushed by definitions you forethought.
Death, as you may apply it, takes the lot,
The drama, deeds, the full house, and the spare
Bedroom where somebody is well aware
Of the assertions that control the plot.
Do not forget that. It will turn up again.
After the worms have gone it will remain.
Though worlds turn round the dead men lie there still.
Do not forget your holiday in Spain.
That is a part of death too, and you will
Find that each moment's grown immovable.

XXXIII.

Those flaming Christians with their hygienic rose
Tattooed upon the lavatory tiles,
Who bend the penis to a sexless pose
And think of childbirth as a sort of piles;
Those gentlemen with asterisks in their hearts,
Those ladies without lamps, those virgin ones
Who don't quite have the conviction of their sins,
They are the negatives where damnation starts.
It is not all in death: there is no end
To the sweating, swivelling consciousness of that loss.
It is in life: to die is to defend
Life by that loss of laboured nothingness.
Those who deny it, though they cannot live,
Possess, but finally, a life to give.

XXXIV.

Evil we unequivocally feel.
It cannot be uptilted, emptied out
Of universes by a sunlit spout.
Remaining emptiness would still be real
And as completely evil. Dead men congeal
In scabs about it: the dying shout,
Their new wounds opening, that they die without
The knowledge that was their part of the deal.
I cannot comfort you. My sins reply.
I cannot speak but in a voice that smears
Evil across the music of the spheres.
You know, as I do, that I too shall die.
Silently then I may wipe out the arrears
Due by an animal in eternity.

XXXV.

Goodness goes on between us but we don't,
Ambiguously though we try to, dare
Define it better than as everywhere
A careful discipline of accident.
It's just not in us now to know what's meant
By the perplexed brocade, the intricate snare
Made of each other's lifetime, which we wear
As an activity or an ornament.
These words go on as we do: hear them preach
Back over every argument to reach
The conclusion of their separate ways of speech.
What they are answered by is what they mean.
Somewhat like them, goodness goes on between
Us and the evil we had not foreseen.

XXXVI.

You will not choose the good or evil way,
But rather truly, as the truest should,
Between two evils each of which is good
Discover what is necessary today.
You will not have the time to stop and stay
Daintily nearby till you've understood
Whether you are the diner or the food
At the long supper on the buried tray.
And yet when all is ready you must choose
From all you've lost which would be best to lose:
Then, having chosen, let the whole world die:
While you, wrapped up in it beneath the land
That rivers wash, winds drag, and roots demand,
Will trail your worlds beyond you through the sky.

XXXVII.

Time is a trespasser here: that the dream survives
The dreamer and this dreaming, that alone,
Or that to waken means the dreamer lives
Although his dream were hollow as a bone.
Either the fable is immortal or
Immortality is itself as plain
A hometruth though of heaven as the brain
Can recognise behind a metaphor.
All the contracting and expanding world
That men make out of what they almost know
Cannot control the prophecies they heard
When shapes of children bickered in their beard
And women silently in choirs below
The cut trunk knelt and saw the dead tree grow.

XXXVIII.

That numerous stranger dipped in my best disguise
Worms his way back over the green hills
Which winds have shaped from beaten miracles
And which old thunderstorms and wells baptise.
He cuts across it home. His light denies
The dark it boasts of, and his step fulfils
The courage of the grassblade that he kills
Dead on the spot he reaches as he dies.
All silence enters him but leaves no trace.
Who is that man who walks without a face
On less than water, on a single word,
On a mere air that whistles its absurd
Jubilant anthem in an elegy's place
Under the agony and is overheard?

XXXIX.

Christ comes to mind and comes across the mind
And ankle-deep like stitches through a wound
Wades words through anger, and He steps behind
The meaning of the movement of the sound
That we had heard as silence. His boulder rolls
Gruffly across our thoughts. Our actions think
Suddenly for us, and the beatitudes slink
Like butlers towards us with His blood in bowls.
All graces air today in the long park
Grass grows more mellow, and our words decay
Into the mystery that we cannot say
As naturally as daylight turns to dark.
We are so close, the world has grown so wide,
That we don't know which one of us has died.

XL.

At last to wish for, fear for what you will,
The world gone out of you and the bones come
Clean to their last supper at the long table.
They eat in darkness. They do not remember
What was their end nor how to count their number.
They let the spade's scenery seep through the hill
Into their marrow, not speaking a syllable.
They do not know by what slow road they came.
They do not even want it kept unknown.
The secret stop. Between the rock and bone
All is in frank silence. And that is why
We think of death in terms of eternity.
Changes obscure the dead but are our own.
They have no way of knowing that they die.

XLI.

And now that the impossible is near,
And after lips, the flimsy hours cajoling,
And after eyes that counted and saw clear,
And before ears are deaf to death bells tolling,
And while the white sheet crumples into grey,
And while the hysterical relatives are kind,
And after having learned the things to say,
And before finding what there was to find,
Shall the calamity without a tongue
Trail voices down, or narrow in the brain
With subtle queries, or run amok among
Those thoughts now slackened by the fact of pain?
Or shall the man, emerging from the torment,
Break through it all and live his dying moment?

XLII.

Dig oars for teeth in. Bruise the rippled hour
That takes you out to where the end takes place,
Then tug apart, by night and final hire,
Lifelong from destiny its half a face.
Behind it bone, and as you shed your wish
To outlast in your journey but in vain,
You'll hear sunshining welcome through the wash
Of the hot body and an hour in pain.
I knew my skull had crossed bones with the womb
(Break bones with teeth till teeth break up like bone)
And that my death was borne within my birth
(Come, feed upon the six walls of my tomb)
And though we prayed together I died alone.
(Lie down beside me and become the earth.)

XLIII.

Dead man, live bogey, living man, I am
Myself an aching shadow, cast between
Corpse and an action; in syntax of the dream
A putrid metaphor for each other man.
Like him in this that I am not the same
But by my singular agony and smile
Distinguished from him for a little while
Although he is more like me than my name.
I've heard you gasping through another's face
In the next room to me, and what I heard
Was my own breathing stopping in your place,
And both of us were listening and were scared:
Yet neither knew that in the other's mind
Danger went out like lightning, pain grew kind.

XLIV

Loquaciously through your selfish agony
You spill out groans across your crumbling room:
Inflexibly emphatic as the tomb,
Silences guide you, for today you die.
Implacably in the right they could reply
When you howl mercy at their apron strings
That, as they take you, you took better things,
A privileged pensioner to your vanity.
Instead of that there's lightning at your door
And silent lightnings nuzzle nearer your
Imagination's bones where they lie bare
Or covered up in brightness worlds below.
A selfish agony is the last place you
Could have expected it—yet it is so.

XLV.

Make after me the contrary image of
A man assailable by the least whim
And there impale perfected seraphim
Anguished by answers truant to their love.
If you have done this then the two disprove
The life of each if both must be the same
And if you give their cancellation name
It will be ghosts you talk of or remove.
Yet in that image if you study it
You'll find your own face written, and learn to meet
Yourself in the immaculate disguise
Of nobody at all without surprise.
Thus you will watch the eternal life awaken.
Can a ghost die? Or nothingness be shaken?

XLVI.

The barrows foundered when the Christian priests
Removed the dead from banqueting by night
In the black belly where digested light
Powdered to nodules, rotted into cysts.
A God, they said, more glorious in His feasts
Than earth in any of our human dreams
Lives in a luminous silence that redeems
The best of men from being the worst of beasts.
And at His table anciently while each
New moment splits into eternity
And men learn all things that no man can teach
They feed on flesh that cannot ever die.
That flesh is His own body: for love it breaks
Up in the hand that takes it, and mistakes.

XLVII.

Already as I parse your life away,
Coiling its ruins round my tortured tongue,
A man of ivy, saying what I say
Through the blown worm-holes that corrupt your lung,
You turn back quietly like a snake on me:
Two fangs edge living out of the dead rubble,
Bud to a bird and settle on a tree
Where double tongues proclaim that truth is double:
That I who die—as you, the living, know—
More of the life I have than yours I lose,
Have come to offer what you dared not choose,
By your death healed when by my own laid low,
Till through the lives that each of us has lent
Death dies in both and songs deny lament.

XLVIII.

I promise you by the harsh funeral
Of thought beleaguered in a spun desire,
And by the unlatched hour, and by the fall
Of more than bodies into more than fire:
And by the blackbird with its throat alive,
And by the drowned man with his tongue distended,
By all beginnings never to be ended,
And by an end beyond what we contrive:
I promise you on an authority
Greater, more sure, more hazardous than my own,
Yes, by the sun which suffers in the sky
I promise you—that words of living bone
Will rise out of your grave and kneel beside
A world found dying of the death you died.

XLIX.

The life I die moves through the death I live
Corrupting even evil with the lie
Of the undying towards eternity:
It lives in fear that is life's negative.
I do not want to go. I will not give
The death I live in to the life I die;
Or trust it will reveal what I deny:
And will not die although I cannot live.
'Take courage, singer,' say your silent limbs,
'You sing of silence but the song that dims
All songs, it washes you and me asleep
And leaves no rumour where a doubt can creep.'
I stop my songs, and stop beside your bed,
And cover up your eyes—for you are dead.

L.

Love listens and redeems. It is the sin
Knocking at some outlandish door within,
Or howling without hope that answer can
Receive it into innocence again.
By love of little things great love's undone,
Yet love of great ones cannot but condone
The extinction of the littleness of man
Which is the source where his great loves begin.
Love hears the sin that is the sin of love
Pleading to be loved, and it loves the sin:
Love hears the hate and the hard words that love
Speaks to its enemy, the love of sin:
And love is silent: silently it streams
Through the continual uproar it redeems.

LONGER POEMS

MARCUS ANTONINUS
cui cognomen erat
AURELIUS

The world is Rome; Carnuntum, on the Danube.

A man seated, a tent, three thousand tents, a man,
His skin sponged brown by the Italian summer,
Darkened by shadows and the sun of Egypt,
A face tugged out by winds of the desert, tight from sea-plod,
Contrary to innocence, and gentle:
The posture harsh; the mind alone is active.
Respectfully his, a boy at the back of him squats:
In front, a skeleton enters
(Epictetus, the wise slave, walks):
Then an Immortal
Staggering upwards painfully under
Bundles, for burden,
Of brown sackcloth wings.
The boy and the skeleton grin and are earnest.
That is their nature. His, the duty;
His, the decision: decide.

There is an army and an enemy,
And one in ten but from which century
He tallies purposes and hears them hold
Clamour raised upon clamour,
Rattle of armour, death squeals.

A mind, erratic within
His decent body, carries
Piecemeal a soul which cannot live outside:
Looks out and vanishes ahead of him.

The boy squats pleasant: truthfully he is blind.
The articulated bones are hollow and unkind.
That is the nature of things. His is the Empire.
His is the duty. Decide.

The boy, a curt word;
The skeleton vanishes.
There, instead of it, stands
(Alive in that curious negligent flesh
He fears for his own)
No master now but his quiet servant.
Words and an officer,
Words, and a name: it was done,
And the hum of despatches begun
Two secretaries scribbling, the couriers off,
And a cold walk in the camp,
And a hot meal, and his duty.

Two hours alone he must sit with the truth,
That bitter gentleman all made of teeth,
Listens to cauldrons and the clank of torture,
Screams from the innocent and the unholy:
Then hearing this he must resign himself,
Prepare himself for action and forget
Warmth, with its quiet
Noise of a woman
Who once breathed beside him,
Cold, with its quiet
Clink of his skeleton's
Vertebrae in him.

It must be done, and it is difficult,
Difficult while soldiers
Aloud about
Tent, bed and table
Query, quip, react
To orders given;
Difficult in his tent,
Difficult in his Empire:
It is difficult to forget and threadbare follow
The thin mind of a slave compelled by masters
To move through all of it without the world.
Beyond all this, he must not ask for comfort.
Others have owned the universe before him

And his destiny yet
Will, fleetfoot, overtake many.

Thus ends his meditation.
Noise, and the tent-flap opens.
Noise, and his name.
He must go out, go sit in judgement,
And he must not make haste.
He ponders quietly and asks quick questions.
Mercy must not itself become unjust.
This can have suicide, but that the gallows,
And one is loaded with new innocence.
He breaks a sword and pushes out in silence.
He had no right to judge them, but a duty.

Officially a banquet, therefore sit
Above the ambassadors and drink wine.
Dim memories recur that take time in
But must be battened or constricted for safeguard
Of his immediate purposes in war.
He smiles attentively. He makes a joke.
A long way gone, but not a long way back
To the boy squatting over difficult sums.
Politely he refuses, makes a promise, then
Singling his enemy confronts the issue.
His empire is about him. His, the duty.
But then go back, and he must be alone,
Prepare for sleep; and it is an emperor's duty
Not to be weary lest he waste his empire:
Barbarians, past the number of sleep,
Wait with long swords for civilisation to nod.
To sleep and not to dream, for in dreams too
Hordes gather against him
And against him bring
That sickness for slaughter
Which history has
Leached into his lineage,
The rattle of armour, death squeals:
And, in his bed, lean hungry longings taunt him,
Pinprick and bite him;

Deep dreams of goodness keep him from sleep.
Why have the heavens not elected him
To be impoverished, alone, unheeded,
Taken all from him but his own mind only
And given him freedom, made him a slave?
O Epictetus! Corpses are moving!
The slave he ambitions
Walks and with humble lessons
Proves the futility of all desire;
Fades in the act, accepting happiness,
The red earth round the oblong of his coffin.
Again the emperor shuts his eyes, and sleeps.
Let no scream from the tortured,
No prim innocence in the reprieved,
No cry against the cupidity of his time,
No pity for men in battle nor for his ancestors under the earth,
No lingering on the loveliness of the flesh,
No hunger after good honour,
Not a single prayer,
Not a hope of mercy
Corrupt the darkness in which he is resting:
Let him lie easily until the morning.

Then, to rise up, punctual not previous.
He puts on dignity like a suit of sack-cloth,
Walks in the weather that is sharp and sad.
He calls his commanders to council.
It is time to prepare
Another ambush.

THE TRANSPARENT PRISONER

They took me somewhere sleeping in the desert
Up middle of a minefield near Benghazi:
And I was hungry—but that was later. At first
It was the Germans—you'd hardly call them Nazi—
Polite and battle-hungry happy men
—O I would like to meet those chaps again.

And everything was decent at headquarters,
After we'd picked our way out like with tweezers,
Decent and capable, and we were ordered
Into small companies, and fed or feasted
Better than back in Cairo. So for ten days
We waited, glad in the shade, glad of delays.

Then we were shifted in a desert truck
Back eighty miles, the sun like liquid steel,
The smell of heat, the nagging—until it took
A hard wrench on my memory to dispel
Those green and English places and the sounds
Which hiccuped at me, festering with old wounds.

But it was still the Germans, and one talked
At great length about his home-town, in what
I soon could recognise as Marburg—talked
And was glad of it, till I let out
A long throng of impatient memories:
Together we mourned the way of instant dies.

There was a Frenchman too—some sort of pilot
In an ugly bandage. The three of us
Got talking, all odd accents, and in a while it
Wasn't just words: we sang the Marseillaise,
The Land of Hope and Glory, and Auld Lang Syne:
Till on that note we reached a little town.

There we changed captors. We were back at base
With I-ties, or Italians, or plain Wops,
Who pinched our watches but could not refuse

To feed us on a diet of their slops.
And it was there that I first learned to sense
The tidy brutality of a barbed-wire fence.

It lay about us, rigorous as the proof
Of human ignorance finally seems to men
—A limiting condition of all life,
Not just of ours—though it was we alone
Who acted camouflage halfways symbol to
It—and the laws we're hourly half-dragged through.

Everything worked by halves, and half-alive,
Half-starved and half-imprisoned as we were,
We were half-tempted almost to contrive
Escapes across that rusting wrestling wire;
But we did not. Instead, half-hearted jokes
Tried to persuade us it was all a hoax.

Then soon it ended, because we moved again,
This time on foot, and I don't really know
How many miles made up the phenomenon
That I describe, though not remembering, now.
Miles anyhow there were, no lack of them.
And afterwards more miles, and still the same.

It was the desert and the sun was high
Or it went down; but it came up again:
A negroid Cyclops or at least his eye,
It pointed at us like an accusing gun
Which would go off if for a moment we
Forgot ourselves so much as to feel free.

Of course we had been guilty; so we went
On, though complaining, yet without arousing
Any emotion that was really meant.
We walked ahead, hypnotized by the horizon:
It wriggled in our sweat, in one round drop:
We did not reach it and we did not stop.

Then the night fell on us whipping us with sand,
The cold, the dry grains in our nose and nails;

The tickling blankets and the loud command
To sleep or wake or empty filthy pails—
—Words in a language that meant no more to us
Than to a bird the fumbled blunderbuss.

We could not sleep, nor wake. We seemed to touch
A secret manifestation of the truth:
We lay down in the desert, and learned to teach
Ignorance to professors: we learned to mouth
Old truths, and to forget them when they hurt,
Hurt us too much: truth became true as that.

We seemed like looking in a dead man's eyes
To see small stars dipped deep in the black pupil,
We'd suddenly and simply realise
How old astrologers could without scruple
Paste our lives on to them and advertise
Their rigmarole as wisdom to the wise.

For they were lying like in a black cup
Tealeaves made out of pure white light might lie
And formed a pattern, and a single drop
Brewed from those fragments of immensity
Could satiate thirst, it seemed, and let us pass
The ghost that most and momently haunts us.

What could have been the banquet of the gods,
I almost wondered, what could it have been
If these stars are the dregs? Are all men besides
Morsels to nibble when the feast is done?
I thought until the thought hardened past pain.
My thoughts grew eyes. They let the stars down in.

So for a long way: but it ended near
Tunis—you know the place. Most of us died
There—but you don't. You never will know where
Tunis pitted the map. It was outside
The squares they plant with pin-marks, beyond the four
Wind's quarters. I lived there. It is everywhere.

You'll reach it through a miserable month,
Sliding on sweat, cartwheeling over vomit,
Climb a few corpses and about the tenth
You'll turn about and think you've reached the summit.
That was your own one, was it? Not at all.
Here is another. You let your foot fall.

Daylight became a sticky mess of flies,
A filthy porridge stewing in our blood,
Lumpy with bubbles, and the rest of us
An ulcer, an excrescence, where they stood
Next me, a second; then they disappeared
And left me as before, and I despaired.

Starvation hits you innerwards like that,
Forces pattern on thought, on feeling, and all
We most think moral in man. It doesn't act
Only. It's something bigger: it thinks. And call
Yourself what you like, the image of God, the True,
Starvation alters reflection. It alters you.

And takes you down with it, through horrid slopes,
Along with shapes, and higher in your brain
It walks and wants, and everywhere escapes
Into its proper hunger, making the mind dim
Over—mere mechanisms built to try
New methods out, try, try to satisfy.

Starvation can lead you to Tunis—the one I know.
It is an old town. There men have lived
Since men have lived, and those who died there knew
That it could hold their bodies, and believed
Others would find a burial ground there too.
I lived there, all of me. Don't go. Don't go.

The stench, the itch, the dysentery, the hours,
And then the moment when the guards brought bread:
I took the lot and gobbled on all fours
And didn't tell them that my mates were dead

Till the thick smell of them and the discoloured face
Made it impossible and I ate still less.

Four men, a breakfast roll, a pail of water,
With at the bottom suds of macaroni,
At least a dozen but about as bitter
As the green slime that rots across a penny.
Hell has its comforts. Those who died forgot
At least the worst of it but I can not.

For life goes on. It keeps on going, going
Over the old hard ground, and the unbroken
Heart breaks again. I felt my life-blood slowing.
Death was at work; when suddenly I was taken,
A slab upon a stretcher, to a ship.
I did not eat there and I could not sleep.

Guns snored from Malta. Planes bounced above my head
The decks and port-holes splashed into the water.
Winds swarmed and hopes subsided. Thoughts went dead;
And hours went pounding hard and helplessly,
Like iron pistons into emptiness.
Then the sea loosened. We had come across.

And then they tended us, gave us to eat
From wholesome plates. We lived in an old castle,
And gradually our limbs at last forgot
They had been hungry. Lips began to whistle,
Fingers to hold a pen, and pain to go.
Thoughts bustled through us, hopefully to and fro.

It didn't last, of course, but nothing does,
And we enjoyed it, knowing it would end.
A train ran weekly and took some of us
Out of it somewhere but I couldn't find
A clue to the direction till one day
I was among the ones who went away.

It must have been two months between the two
Modes of starvation—one, the quick acute

And killing primary need I had come to know.
Death gurgled near it . . . It seemed a mere brute
Rampant and miserable, plunging with a moan
Its whole weight at me: in me like a bone.

The other—but it was in Germany—
A perilous pedestrian sense of God—
It lasted longer, outlasting sun and snow
Two winters and three summers. I watched the slow plod
Of overladen feet, till I had seen
Footprints like letters form an articulate line.

Or rather—but we lived in a tin hut
With one of those long reaches for a prison
Where the slack landscape folding out of sight
Seems to crop up again behind the horizon;
At least we slept there, when we had got through
With hacking coal for sixteen hours a day.

They kept us there for coal, alive enough
To cut it in the dark, but not to think.
They gave us porridge and a kind of dough
Half-baked to bread, and sticky soup to drink.
I ate it, gave them coal, two years and more,
And shivered in a blanket on the floor.

Any conditions continued long enough
Will stretch themselves until a man can live
All of him, in them; and the lowest life
Give highest impulse headroom, though he have
A hutch, a hole, to habit, and
Squalor alone to love and understand.

That is what baffles tyrants. Only death
Can end man's freedom to be all man can.
Prisons are perches. I went underneath
Then came up with a precious undertone
That swirled to song out of the damp dark
Through coughs that came with it and made it stark.

There were enough of them—incarnadined
The shining rock-face with thick frothy spittle,
And hours enough after the coal was mined
To watch how others bended or turned brittle,
Broke in a moment, and the hysteric calm
After the black barred ambulance had come.

Yet in the tunnel, at the rock-face, when
Accumulated by exhaustion, thoughts
Would form and fold and hold themselves close in
About the point of peace, were other states.
The shift, twelve hours had gone, and six more yet.
The pick-axe slithered in my hand like sweat.

Huge blocks and boulders mined off hours ago
Would seem a sick weight, and my stomach turned
Into a sob, and memories of snow
And footprints tapering backwards through it burned,
Like tiny monosyllables, blaze with fear.
My weak arms worked. I seemed to disappear.

Lying along my belly, the rock roof
Two feet above, the wet rock floor upon
My muscles sliding, I seemed to grow aloof
From my own body or to grow a skin,
Flesh, form, and senses, deep within my own
And to retire to live in them alone.

My hands against the coal would grow transparent,
Then, like a match felt softly by its flame,
My arms would char into a wandering current;
Warm radiance crept up them till the same
Vivid transparence flooded every part
And I could see the beating of my heart.

As sedentary worms that burrow in
A froth of sand cement it with a slime
Out of their own skin, I too shed my shine
On to the rock below me till in time

It took the same transparence as myself:
I saw its seed, its kernel, through the filth.

And then above, the rock like catching fire
Bled into clearness to the pointed grass
That bled beyond it; and the sun that higher
Winds in its web this planetary mass
Grew clear; stars stood above it, and ranged behind
Its brightness like the workings of a mind.

I saw the moments and the seasons swim
Precisely through me and I saw them show
Huts, hills and homes, the distance, and my dream
Of little footsteps shrieking in the snow
As they tip into darkness, all grow bright
And smother everything in transparent light.

I watched. A tender clarity became
That moment mine, as clear as through a hand
Bones shadow out into a candle's flame
And tender-terrible as to understand
Faults that the finding of has often killed
Pity and pain in you, fault-ridden child.

And I acknowledged. O I don't know what,
But greater grace than my acknowledgement
Could ever reach the edge of, or forget—
A tender clarity that would not relent
Till I saw mercy from the merciless brink
Of thoughts which no mind born was born to think:

A tender clarity that is not understood
But by the helpless in a dangerous instant,
A perilous deity. O my good God,
Come quietly at last, and become constant.
The years grow small about me. I despair.
Impose your order on my every hour.

It was an order, yes! but not imposed
Though not within itself complete, and not

Abstract—an order, movement, force, composed
Of situations, things, which one great thought
Transparented completely through its mind
To light long images laid down behind.

I was at mercy of them, am unable
Ever to meet except set in dismay
No, no, not shadows—but the implacable
Splendour descending, splitting tenderly
Skin, skull, and atom, till, though merely man,
I recognised a reason for all pain.

I saw the world, the world in full transparence,
Stark peaks through earth like vultures crowding down,
Become a symbol for its own appearance,
A system that completely and unknown
Was worked through by old forces and old laws
Which let it mean them, being what it was.

No other certainly. It didn't change
But stayed as still as in the stifled heart
Feelings not spoken, words would disarrange,
Can lie in hiding for their counterpart.
It was the world. Confuse no heaven nor hell.
The boring bubbling world you know so well.

The cold unclean and comfortable world,
Hard as an anvil, pointed, and as flat;
Circular saw, the orbit, square sphere swirled
Through bones, through brains; the spotted speedy spate
Of rivers, riders, racing with a will
Past men and mountains through the inexplicable.

Lying along my belly in the mine,
Or labouring footprints in the German snow,
I, the involved one, learned to love again
And, loving it, attempted to reach through
To the broad air, the people, though for years
My pit-prop prison peopled unawares.

84

I learned to love the self-same world as now:
For love of it, though its transparency
Was my captivity. I planned carefully how
To reach through to it and in it to be free.
I killed a man. I killed him and escaped
Into it living. Then, at last, I wept.

I got away through the Bohemian South
And into Yugoslavia where I joined
A band of partisans who lived next to death.
In that excitement, thinking was postponed
Or sharpened hard on the best ways to kill.
I kept myself alive, and that was all.

But now as years pass and the war is done
I find myself of evenings often enchanted
And, guessing what goes on within my brain,
Conceive myself as of a being haunted
By corpses more alive than his own flesh:
They dog me with a brittle tenderness

That breaks upon a whim, but nothing breaks
Through my continual sense of loss and sense
Of being cut off by simple slight mistakes,
Everyday errors, from an innocence
That is still mine though it lives a life apart
Folded transparently in the transparent heart.

BIOGRAPHY OF AN IDEALIST
The Crystal and the Shadow

No wise humorous man
To light a frowning pipe,
But somewhat pedant-lipped:
Too thin yet over-ripe,
In thoughtful candour he
Stood an inch from the Throne.

He didn't like the king
But thought it cruel to kill
Unless, of course, there was
A matter of principle.
He knew his mind and that
Saints are a shabby lot.

The law was not for them,
The human dispensation;
Unwholesome justice or
Mere moral sanitation.
Saints could not be condemned
By systematised sin.

Their dreams were all exact
Replicas of Love,
Creations of the Creator,
The labour of the Dove.
No thought of man upset
Their regent symmetry.

His radiant mind performed
Its intricate perfections,
Illuminating summer
With brilliant bold rejections.
Childhood pursued him with
Ascetic ferocity.

Yet old enough to know
The bitterness of not

Distilling what is best
Out of the least thought
—Because there was the king,
A distracting energy.

A saint's shabbiness dresses
Gutters and colonnades,
And bustling stock-exchanges,
And the bare Queen of Spades,
Annoyances and sorrows,
Brash friendships and lush quarrels,

All are dressed in white
Patterns of dentilled silk
By men with lice in their hair
Who live on a diet of milk:
And yet the king despised
Rags, ulcers and bones.

He knelt before a monk:
I never quit this place.
A hermit answered him:
The mirror burns the face.
All night the stars were dark.
Dreams perfected his heart.

They came in harmonies,
Their courage crisp; they came
With tabors, flutes and drums
Brocading their acclaim
With wild handclapping of
His regent symmetry.

They came on stilts or, dwarfed
By insolent windmills, came
In figure S processions
As agile as a flame:
They came out of the black
Night of his white pillow.

Dancing, turning up
With ancient cut-throat facts,
They bargained hell for leather
That the damned might not relax:
Limbs were lashed to the dance
With sacred cow-hide.

Their motley measured mind's
Capacity to defy
The shades of startled lightning
God fastens in the sky:
And when thunder followed
He knew the time had come.

The king was counting money
And heads of corn and men,
Thinking the matter over,
And counting them again.
His tally was a small
Part of the passing world.

He knew the time was wrong
Although as right as rain,
As right as rain or thunder
Or water on the brain:
He counted out his money
And counted on his men.

Their weaknesses he knew:
Poverty kept him awake
Arguing that he had
Enough money to make
Their imperfections serve
His own imperfect ends.

The king surveyed his kingdom,
Following paper clues,
Historical documents and
Clippings of recent news.

The king frowned at his ledger.
His shadow danced on the wall.

A shadow's colour is
Inconstant consistency,
Half made of shape, half light,
And all transparency:
A shadow has the form
Of a very cool mirror.

The king was quick to think
Of evil in the wall,
And evil cancelling evil;
But the result of it all
Was still as evil as
Evil ever was.

The king was quick to learn
That what his shadow did
Expressed his best intention:
He therefore never hid
Within the light or ran
Away from his own shadow.

The king encased in light
Watched his shadow grow
Under the stern sunlight
Or in the lamplight's glow.
The king frowned at his ledger.
His shadow danced on the wall.

But someone else was watching,
Hidden within the light
Of his knowledge of the shabby
Soul of the king that night,
In thoughtful candour he
Stood an inch from the Throne.

An universe in crystal
Implored him to imply

By his ideal devotion
Its regent symmetry:
God in His heavens fertile,
Lightning lashed to the sky.

Lightning without a shadow
Yet not in a vacuum,
Completing the crystal's
Equilibrium,
Solidifying light
In every solid body.

Even the crystal dark
Lapped shadows from the lake
And obscure constellations
Groped about to make
Absence achieve perfection
In the blackest art of night.

Illuminated by
The inside of a dream
That casts no shadow and
Only an ideal beam,
The action in the crystal
Penetrated the brain.

'Now, king, the time has come.
The saints you scorned are free
To establish in your kingdom
The regent symmetry
Of man to man that is
An image of God's body.

'Prepare to lose tonight
Substance and shadow and
The sleek and timid falsehoods
You used to keep your land.
The honest worm will nurse
Her young at your breast-bone.

'You've changed the laws of man
And made the laws you break
But the Law of God will never
Alter for your sake.
Your flesh will decompose,
Your soul disintegrate.

'A man of bits and pieces,
Believing this and that,
An athletic ventriloquist,
A spiritual acrobat,
Your fall means that each thought
Will burn in a separate fire.'

The king looked at his shadow
As it swung round the room.
The king looked at his killer
And prepared to meet his doom.
He coughed to clear his throat:
'Ah, so at last you've come

'The years have been too long.
I can remember when
I thought your saints at least
As good as common men.
I should have died before
I lost respect for them.

'Perhaps I am unfair.
I die a usual death.
A traitor must be friendly
And pretend to good faith.
For myself, I never was
Above dissimulation.

'If I believed at all
I believed in the small mistake
In judgment or behaviour
That only men can make,

The perfect limitation
Breached by imperfect power.

'My evil cancelled evil.
Your good will cancel mine.
The limits of a shadow
Are difficult to define.
But the meaning of a maggot
Is that it has to dine.'

They led the king away.
They shot him just as dawn
Was beginning to cast long shadows
Over the royal lawn.
The saints were counting money
And heads of corn and men.

Ideals that grow like crystals
Concentrate energy
In parallels and prisms,
Contracting fluency
Into the symmetry of
The soul's geometry:

The soul that casts no shadow
Indicates human grief
With intricate lightning: but
God is beyond belief.
The shadow in the crystal
Is that there is none.

The saints are counting money:
Merely regent now,
Lopsided without shadows,
They cannot tell us how
The king within the mirror
Came by his pious gestures.

God is beyond belief:
His image everywhere

Half made of shape, half light,
Establishes despair.
The saints are counting money
Because the saints are men.

THE COMING OF THE GRAIN

And spare your tears. For I am one
To whom the sun's each practice shone
Against the coming of the grain.

On my deathbed I shall repel
All courtesies. I'll make my will,
Through the drizzle of northern nightfall, call.

I'll leave the daylight to proud women:
Birdsong embroidered from collar to hem
To witty lads who sleep with them.

And the night like iodine
With its sharp purples, felt not seen,
To wounded and to desolate men.

I owe a debt to circumstance
Which in a woman was too kind once.
That debt is my son's inheritance.

Let me be poor. That debt will last
Till all the profit of her breast
Is paid in pain and pain is past.

I take upon me the heavy day
And, millstone-necked by what I see,
I grind all chaff, all straw away.

Undo life's delicate miracle
And let low organisms fall.
To me the part means more than the whole.

I *am* a part, and that's my function,
I'm not eternity's extreme unction,
And I must be taken in close conjunction

With whisky, females and income-tax laws,
Not with the final or primal cause.
I follow nothing but my own nose.

This is the hard beginning, here
And now, and high and dry, near
To nothing but beginning's fear;

Head and shoulders above the town,
Lonely, going against its grain,
Quietly, like a dying man.

Out of the house I look back now
Over whoever that man was who
Sat on the high stool filled with straw.

Far outdistancing metaphor
I fight without any commotion or stir
At table and chair behind the door,

Fight to make me an instrument
Of bright proportions, austere and bent
Upon nothing other than all men want.

The poetry is an incident
Forced upon men who take the hint
And say no more than what is meant.

The poetry must not matter now
When freedom is a circus show
Which only those on the tight-rope know.

Out of the belly love of brutes
A chaos chuckles and darkness shoots
Over the lanky scaffoldings' lights.

A million interruptions fall,
Each more little, each more still
Than a man climbing a climbing hill.

This is the night of terrible souls
Strayed from their branches, night that fulfils,
In panic's disorder, the tenderest kills.

And I under a lonely roof,
Look back, writing the calendar off,
Look back down the day as long as a life.

Look back among the blessed faces
Scattered together in books of addresses
And write wherever truth digresses.

Laid lowly there on the carpet where prayers
Bow down and ask for nothing, fear
Only promises and forgive despair.

I shall be better able then
To know what all these small things mean,
My seat of straw, the skeleton,

This monstrous pity for myself
And him, the meaning of the filth
We fight, and our proud duty's wealth.

Out of the level-headed ruin,
The burden of the afternoon,
Girls like choruses sung out of tune.

Out of it all, I now come back
Paid by the poor and healed by the sick,
I, the accusers, come back and speak.

Against the city's side-tracked wheels
The fools who rise, the blood that falls
With an artillery of vowels.

Upholster Hell and Heaven too.
Let them divide us when we're through.
Put me wherever he cannot follow.

Out of the coffin's wooden breast
To accident let him be cast
One with those labourers without rest.

Spare your tears. He is a man
For whom the sun to no purpose shone,
Who took the name of life in vain.

Let him continue it and spend
Eternity in his mankind.
At work in dung with pigs of the mind.

Or here explode him out of sight
Pump bullets through all those who fight
On the wrong side of the heart.

Let us be white blood that heals
While on a carpet of upright nails
The angel of the tramcar kneels.

Yellow and white are our only colours.
We are Samson robbed of his pillars.
We must be mad to kill our killers.

The aching sympathy of the flesh
Unwinds me towards him till I wish
I could allow our bodies to touch

Once in mutual forgiveness, once.
No! Hush that word's extravagance!
There's no forgiveness for this dunce.

For then, he smiles . . . the boss . . . the big
Blue smile, a cold animal hug.
This is the hole those shadows dug.

My grave, and his grave too, the grave
Of all the world, and of love,
The grave that none will ever leave,

None will outlive. I feel the smile
Strutting and cold and pitiful
With its rank ceremonial.

All this is platitude and the small
Hot porcelain the crucible
Of song, exactly beautiful,

Is wept on, watered, trodden down.
We, the singers, are desperate men.
Our guns are forgeries. We burn

Our locks. They are our enemies.
The words we use are filled with spies
That turn the truth like milk to lies.

And to escape all this we run
Into extremities alone
'Amantio dispositio non.'

The platitudes are everywhere
In speech itself, and poetry mere
Jargon of felons mouthing their hair.

Yes, we are Hamlet. Straw
Against the grain, unnatural, dry,
Salt carcasses within the sea.

Then at lunchtime stop and totter
Among the street fogs thick
Streets where even the wind seems to stutter.

But often in the tram I hear
Between the clattering stumble of years
Birdsong forcing entrance there.

Birdsong, that sharp embroidery
Of chirruping straw in the dovetailed sky
Or needling pollen pinned to a tree.

Then the world's an aqueduct
That catalytic metals tricked
Into the properties of luck.

The work gathers about my joy,
The birdsong like a battle cry
One way directs its scattered flow.

Then I return to rough and tumble,
The magazines' names with which I fumble,
The boss who butts in with gossip and grumble.

Out of the grunt and the tramcar's snort,
Stagger of signs and the motor's retort,
Glides the good angel high as a fort.

He passes and his steps repeat
Flower by flower, note by note:
Like a carpet through the street.

Power and pattern beyond law.
I, on my dry green stool of straw
Am crouched like a prayer for what I saw.

Then the corn, the new machines
That thresh it wonderfully fine,
All these return and each alone.

Shovels at ankles, picks at waists,
This daily congregation rests,
Made out of bones deformed with cysts.

Rests for a while where each one digs
Pitfalls to parcel whirligigs.
All are weary: none relax.

The grunt of horns, the sear of brakes,
Girls like tunes through humdrum blocks
Are audience. The guilt awakes.

To mend the disorder that dotes in my mind
He comes in the homely way of mankind
Smashing the wind's vase in his hand.

Then the daylight largely wasted,
Then the darkness never tasted
Joy the sorrow ill-digested:

Gurgle of straw in clotted stream,
Scanty skeleton's anger, shame
These in refrain beneath the dream.

These come back his voice to be
And fix attention heavily
Upon the loss within the lie.

Then the face's twisted pain
That once seemed happy in disdain,
Looks like vagrants, tracked down, moved on.

Then the canvas crammed with straw,
Mattressed bunks for men who die,
The grain ripped from them dry and raw.

Foreign words make heavy weather
And city streets chime at the end of their tether
A lovely community chancing together.

So that the place of my ink-stained desk
Is taken by storm to a straw-built nest
On the crest of a world just after the next.

But not for long though it is late.
Forever! For people come with their teeth white set
Into the smile against the heart,

Hurry their ways upon me, make
Small conversation mine. I take
My part and space diminishes back.

Come with cakes, small hours of talk,
Riot and righteousness and talk,
Talk until space diminishes back.

Into the street, the hallmark place
Of everything's slick use screen kiss
Where nothing could be better or worse.

Out of the street like a hunch-backed sailor,
Duck-gaited, badly in need of a tailor
Wobbles the fly-weight prophet and killer.

He stamps about like a Sunday tripper,
Posts his name on my blotting paper,
Bamboozles me, then butts in like a copper.

My high green stool is filled with dust,
With powdered straw I seem to taste
As I undo the parcels addressed

Some from the shop across the road,
Some from the ocean's other side,
All to the firm by which I'm paid.

Out of the packages' brown-paper names
Emerge a messenger footed on thumbs,
A voice that struggles like straw that swims

To take stock of the distant places
Scattered together in books of addresses
That are alive with people's faces.

He comes in the homely way of mankind
Post-marked through space and pigeon-brained
When space breaks out of its vase with the wind.

From Teneriffe to Maryhill,
Stark additions of names that fall,
Thornliebank to Aix-la-Chapelle.

Out of the sensual habit of truth
Daily the man comes discoursing with
Neither glib usage nor purpled mouth.

He is whatever man I meet:
I was no other: he is what
Happens to me each day I sit

In the quiet corner like
A small child riding a borrowed bike
Among the other people's books.

There is no end to him except
A token payment of our debt
With all of my life remaining yet.

Beginning the day I arrive late
And more of my apologies fit
The smile of excuse with which I am met

And the bright aftermath of sorrow
Not in an ounce the splendid universe
Will bail out cargoes or its tides reverse.

At the divide of compartments of rust:
Or those light-headed that trump up lust
In films, in football, the name of Christ.

Or poetry or politics, anything else
That is used to level the high-handed kills,
Presumptuous prayers or the drunk to the gills.

It's no use scolding the world. It's better,
Older than us, and maybe we clutter
Its broad-toned language with our stutter.

Look behind the curtain of prayer
With these wide eyes that open like doors
Into fulfilment everywhere.

Spare your tears. He is a man
For whom the sun's each practice shone
Against the coming of the grain.

And on his deathbed he repels
All courtesies. He makes his will;
Because I go against the grain.

Out of the happenings of truth
Without glib usage or purpled mouth
I come describing my daily youth.

The revelations have another place,
This is for office hours. I trace
The continual crisis of growing wise.

Perhaps a little pompous, yet
Years are as difficult a debt
To leave unpaid and we need to admit.

Beginning from the place I work
With magazines and such-like muck,
Scholarly rubbish heaped up dark

Round the intellects of men
Whose illuminations harden again
For the doom of death and the death of pain.

By nicotined lamplight and loggerheads
I go goodbying and meet instead
The jumbled traffic of homecoming bodies.

The high constructions of daylight dim,
Birdsong fades out, the girls don't hum
But are glad-eyed over with eyes like a thumb.

I have a debt to circumstance
For it was kind in a woman's glance.
The debt is my son's inheritance.

The lovely community chancing together
Where foreign names make heavy weather
And city streets shine at the end of their tether.

That's all I have but that will last
Till the whole profit of her breast
Is paid in pain and pain is past.

For me the part is more than the whole.
I *am* a part and that's my function.
I'm not eternity's extreme unction
And I must be taken in close conjunction.

GROUND PLAN FOR A CHURCH

Façades come later. The designer uses
The first rib that Adam ever had
And carves it with exactly the same instrument
As once carved chaos.

To keep at it, to keep at it, that's the trick;
To forget about crockets, bosses, quadripartite vaults,
Limiting delineation to nave, choir and transepts
And simple arithmetic.

To keep infinity out and the exciting gradients
Elevations presume when they're not measured in
Terms of underlying ditches, ruts if you like,
The human medians.

A church is built to contain people,
A population container: and yet it is meant to be
One place at one time,
Time's staple.

You too are aware that every man lives
In a different place from every other
And is surrounded by different patterns of time,
Disparate ogives,

And that a coincidence in the desultory
Movement of legs and backsides can never
Range two men side by side
In the consistory.

So it becomes necessary to devise a space
That will condense their movements to one time only
Not conflicting areas of experience, no, not above all
The human race.

The species is definable, zoologically delimited
And reasonably distinct:

But the reason itself arranges the very partitions
That must be assimilated.

The reason itself is an historical asset
Conditioned by its own transcriptions of the evidence.
This church must be built of a sort of stone that will
      contradict history
Or, better, by-pass it.

Old stones, if they are hard, are best for this. They have
Brought their origin forward to the point where
Change is unlikely, so that their history
Must behave.

And ground too should be carefully chosen
So that it is always pitched plumb centre on the horizon
Where sunset and sundown, for different men,
Mix in one orison.

Each shrug of the earth must be synchronised
At the level of the foundations.
But there must be no Euclidean lines on the drawing board,
Nothing idealised.

Each detail matured slowly like good wine,
An immediate exactitude in the general proportions,
Numerals as part of the aesthetic evidence, all drawn
Into complete design.

For this house is meant as man's guest house for God
As creation is God's for man.
It is needed because the human animal cannot
Be understood

Except, perhaps, when a long reconciliation
Between him and his God is broken by
Immediate quotidian proximity
And the resultant retaliation

Of God through the knowledge of sin that His presence brings
Against sins forever forgotten:
So that man knows the sin of his knowledge and sings
In praise and terror of such things.

It is necessary, therefore, that the building should not
        interpret.
It should simply be of such dimensions as will contain
Men
And God should be able to sleep quietly in the transept.

Perhaps, after all, the Mosaic Tabernacle,
Its nomadic agility substantiating an ubiquitous God,
Brought time to a standstill and, since then,
All has been architect's prattle.

Certainly the Heavenly Examiners
Have given few signs of being satisfied by
The various foundations laid down by our designers
And raised to the sky.

Perhaps, of course, we have been too modest.
Perhaps we have not believed with enough fervour
That, however badly our building was conceived,
It was still our best.

We laid our plans too low.
We did not understand
That everything we do
Is always true.

In the end our church cannot stand too high.
Once drawn, the thin boundaries may be steepled
Up to whatever pinnacles our engineers can warrant
As strict possibility.

THE GENTLE ENGINEER

I.
Then, taking the bit of his blood between those molar
Masses of nerve, his brain thrashed from the sky
  An incipient energy,
  And trussed space into solar
Configurations of all time, above all making, among all
Cuboid or perpendicular planes or facets, all sorrows, all well.

  So to these tales
  The town stands up
  At intervals
  That cannot stop:
  And no room's here
  For a root's tip
  To stab one layer
  Of slate or concrete,
  No water to suck
  In the paved street:
  There is no way back.
  We, therefore, here
  Must search that dead
  Beginning, before
  Roots raised a bud,
  Before the planets
  Sundered, the first
  Fall of the sun;
  When hot rain burst
  The intermediate
  Nothingness
  To mineral seed
  That fostered us.

Before that we were lost, because then made
Out of a lack, even of atmosphere,
  From a dissection of zero
  Planted and pieced, perfected.
Yet the stallion stampeding into direction through all that is,
         never continues, leaving

Us daily less lost, more perilously absent, less neighbour to
                                        nil and more grieving.

I do not know the gods.
I did not reap gold corn
With Ceres, nor with Herod
Suffer infection long.
Krishna was absent from
Those battlefields where I
Saw men and screaming women
Die and die and die.
Even in dreamy fictions
Visiting angels never
Gave explicit directions
On where lay my law-giver.
Now in this city here
Limousine wheels revolve.
An aeroplane is astir.
War is a safety valve.
A lady shares my settee.
I'm liked by good-humoured snobs.
A policeman prowls his beat.
Smooth women guard small cribs.
A drunken scientist nods.
The poor die and the rich.
I do not know the gods.
Here there is merely much.

I, who've begun to lose my life already,
(I had begun at that first sundering
    Of nebulae to starlings)
    Might one day drop these tidy
Trammels off, and coffin make a cockpit of all nowhere,
                                        might
Lose life to what no life yet has to die, and so keep godly
                                        state.

The adaptation, perhaps, is new,
But the old wish still drags after traces
Of blood at daybreak, the huntsman's halloo

Still sounds, his leathery hound still races.
Busily we are scaffoldings
Gauntly and gracefully inset where
The planetary desert rings
With hammer and song and the riveting fire
That yet may let us be taken down
To unveil unpeopled our quiet construction.
So I make hope of bricks, and grin
Past atoms at my skeleton.
Yet with my sensible elbow, I
Can feel the heated crowds, their kind
Peripheral anxiety
Prodding, perplexing, heavy, blind.
O woman walking with your child
Past the placard about eternal life!
O gentleman long-since grown bald
With keeping wolf and werewolf off!
O child, you cry in your warm bed
What would you do if as you spoke
Death's intricate abracadabra made
Your mattress fossiliferous rock!

Immediate masses interpose between
Our origin and end, and no root's tip
    Can pierce that dark for vapour,
    Condensing grains of stone.
We, who are further from zero than flowers, gapped up and
                    off from that first dead
Beginning, nestle away from it and draw nearer to one another's
                        warm side.

Yet it was we built mountains into gods.
The curriculum of creation invented by
Our earnest ancestors, fits elsewhere with
The facts we are. Here this city gently
Makes ghosts of them, and offices marry us
Away from the appalling intimacy
Lonely ones hold with what they heard of. O when
Will Genesis, that chill song scantily
Muffled for love or the nunnery, once more cling

To the naked charmed imagination of
The most of us? Nearer that neighbour than
Woman or man can come, which made nought noun
And, without pedigree, begot and gave birth
To all that time contains but cannot comfort.
Houses take turns to hide us from the clouds,
Women from lightning, but their sheltering weakness
Does not enchant the intruder off. Look,
Where the town stands up, cheerful postcards encircle
Grief the poor ghost, industrious schedules dig
A superstitiously obstinate wall against
The winter. Death like the seed of ebony
Comes from strange parts. But in the conscious heart
Lives on a wayfarer towards the other end
Who with hard footsteps and hoarse voice can leave
A genial blessing that is no reprieve.

II.
Light changes. Standing on a sidewalk
I, under stars, an orrery, feel
Cold winter swarm possessively towards me, or
Hear from my bleak position its sound.
Roots crystallise. Their cell walls shrivel.

Hear too, a remote insinuation on wheels,
The deed, the speed, the fruit of metal,
One car that whispers gently by
To leave the snow that locks about my feet.

This is a street and that the moon
On its high stool knock-kneed
In oblong petticoats; a sheet of light
Left to drape over me as round a nerve
Is white fat tightly closing.
Overhead the blackboard in the sky is grey.

I, in an ignorance equal to
Each solitary potential's moving
From the periphery inwards

Towards the brain, I carry
Messages that I cannot
Understand or amend.

Snow only and no stars is what I see.
I hear a motor's snort.
And what I smell is dried-up ice.
I taste the nicotine in my own saliva.
Nothing moves for me to touch
On this hooped tightrope that is world but I.
So touch and taste me, see, smell, hear me, world,
That we may know each other and be known.

Light sags beneath the invisible stars. Clouds drag
Like driftnets, ready, heavy to haul, low clouds
Entangled in tall spires. The snow banks up,
A slippery furnace. Well, readily, I
Will go, if I must, across the sleek and snoring
Automobile-driven, I don't know who it's by,
Makes snow sulk over us, a purse of ice.
Maybe too I will still, if the white fall
    Accumulates to become
    My dream in telegram,
Take roads on broadly as a way of knocking
Lights up in a quick, perhaps splendid, moment
Doorbells can bring us from inquisitive boys.
But, as it is, and the distances make little
Of all my haste, I move alone in this street
And meeting no-one, trouble none.

At this time, however, and as I move, my eyes
Pick bones from houses and crush skeletons
Up in round tears and flat glances, fragmentary
Molars of an imagination. Polish me bright
Earth, mother, kieselguhr!
Polish my eyes, you scraps of a planet!
Winterly and essentially you are
An awkward spread of
Rockwork, roadwork, paintwork, work and
Distances where my always autumnal

Traffic can cross: stuffed schedules frozen into wax
Melt down to fruit; they drop; they rot.

Whatever moves moves towards its end to end
Meeting its own newcomer from the cold.
I cannot move towards where but whither from.
And that perhaps is why herein I remember
The stale odour of summer,
Dancehalls where men, the capillaries of event,
Small people in lipstick or
Lounge suits swell beneath
A saxophone's blue shudder.
Yes, that is why I pass
Places peripheral
To the capital.
Silence is central. Operations deploy
A continual person I am
About and against his own best calm.
I tether geese to these walls.
Contra barbaros ducent
Handbills, handouts,
Toothpaste, resurrection,
Only, all only, today
Pursued with the vigour of spring.
I cannot see it but I look at what.
If she could live that lady would be blind
(Who is my love, who has my love),
She whom I build from eyes
At every angle of head and body,
She whom I would, who would herself, see clearly
Past barrier and distraction
The quick of existence.
I convict her, a crystallising witch,
Of sackcloth and ashes out of her worms.
She is not there who does not therefore,
And only a corpse lies nakedly still while we watch it.
It is her bones that powder with my glances,
As I move down this street that cannot move
Toppling I talk, my projection sidling away from
Streetlamp to streetlamp. Like towards negative

An impulse in a nerve moves on a brain
I tackle my pattern to this stone street.
It does not move. My shadow vanishes.
Another action blurs those images.
And I move on a little distance, instructing
My shape on the sidewalk behind me
'Here you are simple. Here you can be forgotten.'
Yet somewhere I know that spaces are interdependent.
Dimensions do not die.
The schoolma'am moon,
A spinster with parched breasts,
A swollen blackboard and a countless sum,
Hold me up straight on guy-rope lights:
Or else, unsteadily,
The outline of a head
Will rock over phenomena
And burn its lesson on stone.
I will not hence who will not henceforth.

Then at this point of continuous passage I learn
How action, the plausible vagrant,
Will not be stopping tonight,
Will not be stopping.
I see men sliced into hands.
They are locked in a purse of ice
And their disembodied activities
Roam in a noose or whirl
Winds against cauterised walls.
For when I move, the distance moves beside me.
The distance moves, the separation stays.
I am in this street. I move on the capital.
But though they lead these streetlamps cannot follow,
And though I move I cannot stay behind,
Perpetual as they would seem to be.
The fat man Space and his thin brother Time
Travel in my compartment, and I know
The cards are stacked against me. I will lose
An eternal soul to those continual thieves.

The roots go down that they may up again.
I am in this street. I move on the capital.

Polish my body with sandstone fretting, and with
Arrows fermenting from
Windows onlooking
A glance in love of this night,
Make it serene to consummate torture and
Remember the sun,
The mincing sound of water
With waterhens in the evening of moods once my own.
Hurdling synapse, that memory makes translation
By difficult language inform
And evolve itself into
The signal I see in the smile of a strange young moment.
Not action, but reaction, wisely then.
Remember the sun as it was,
Back in the summerlight.
This street of stones reacts to that memory.
The moon casts down flat brilliance.
Arid turbulence falls apart
And a belligerent mass
Of the silence in this street
Intrudes with its clean perspective
Over me,
That through me, by ecdysis,
In dropping of masks,
As dropped-off leaves,
The skin come clean away,
The five roots of the tree of knowledge vanished into
An ultimate focus,
There may be sympathy and my acceptance,
Loving this gaunt good street of stones like sunlight.

Let me, as orrery, be lightened towards
The insinuation of eyes that have seen shoals
Of the resurrected into tranquillity moving
Towards destinations that they carry on.
Polish my speech. Polish my words, you winds,
You undulations of sorrow, O scrawny street,

You bricked-up chimneys, abrupt clangs of a tram,
Teach me to speak, you exact observations.

Moving out down away far towards
Whatever capital you lead me to, I'll carry
As the thin nerve-cell to the brain and sinews
What you make into me of your own nature.
Long fingers of light, or is it
Chalk? powdering up before me, as the moon
Scribbles her giant handwriting across
Roofs and the dark grey sky,
Open my insight to
The elements of direction.

To move, yes, never away but always towards,
That is my destination.
Distance unravels within me. My taste buds surprise
Odorous sauces wrapt in the tang of a snowflake,
A curt rough brittle snowflake.
A gentle contagion alternating
Upwards through barriers energies spin
Correctly around the prisms, pinacoids, domes,
Each of its crystal facets, and around
The liquid walls, dissolving roofs and rafters
I am made up of, by strange architecture,
Infects us both, this crystal and myself,
With all the history existence has.
Immense intrigues embroider this instant with
The reactions of eras; pterodactyls lumber:
Ancient limpets are embossed on rock:
An oceanic sludge creeps into life:
The principals of matter find each other:
This flake and I converge from all beginnings.

I move across. I am made up upon
At every instant by a ton of bricks,
Cement and polished sandstone, granite blocks.
And fossils spun from powdery chalkmarks burn
Beneath my eyelids in the cold white night.

It is my own blood nips at every pore
And I myself the calcified treadmark of
Process towards me:
All of a million delicate engines whisper
Warm now, to go now
Through dragnets of tunnels forwards as my life.
I carry that which I am carried by.

It is this street at last has rubbed the layers,
Those static concretions of eyes, an observer's,
And wrinkles flattened, the mock objectivity,
So that I meet in my least, impoverished impulse
Enormous autonomies I come to dread,
And then accept as each involves away
Uncounted interdependencies in space:
And in my roots like sweet quick sap
Knowledge comes up through capillaries of reaction
And I know not what it was not I knew.

Eyes slacken. Words go down.
My seven senses yawn.
An old man, tardily
Past need of them, I
Am the skulking ground of tarsus, foot, hoof, wing-tip,
And dinosaurs with cobbled heads, their legs,
Crawl out about me to become my witness.

It is like death to lose thus the dear body.
It lies, a tangle of insidious knowledge
Across this traffic course.
I knew a girl, and with her warm wet mouth
She kissed a corpse awake,
And when the corpse with open lips assented
And hard hands held her and
Her head went back, her head went blank. She loved.
She has a house of level grass and is
A lesson on geography, unlearnt.
And that is death and that is what comes down
At every turn from stones I move among.

For I no longer know who moves nor why
More than my nerves know what they tell my eye.

This is a street and that the moon
But I do not know how nor when.

A maze of energies, dextrously from a dozen
Planes, planets and pinacoids swivel at once.
I carry on, but what I carry is
All these to where I do not know they take.
Distances whisper like a sleek motor car
High out ahead of me, and will not stop,
Will not stay steady till they are attained.
No action is possible. Only reaction permits
Untidy wisps of direction to float out.

An impulse in an enormous
Structure of round white light
I spin off through it at
The touch of rock, the touch
Of this street, against and over
And off through it towards . . .

The moon watches,
Peppery, livid.
And action will not
Be stopping tonight.
Action will
Be going on.
Action will never
Come to rest
Nor ever be mine
By my own act.
The centuries go on beneath my breath.

The moon shivers as her bare white arms
Dangle uncertainly down between gables.
I cross the road, quietly underneath,
Towards the warm width of a wall in the cold night.

Lights waver off on either side. My shadow
Bites the black asphalt from its sleeve of snow.

III.
'Hello! Hello! . . . What's that? of course it's me.
I got your telegram, and really I
Just don't know what you hope that I will say . . .
What's that? Don't say it then? . . . But Mary, Mary,
I must get this across. I must sincerely
Try to get over to you that he's why
I'd sooner shoot myself than have you marry . . .
It's not myself . . . It isn't isn't me
I'm looking after but I know what you . . .

It's absolute spring madness. Why not try
Pretending you've lost money. I'll guarantee
If you were broke you'd see him wince away . . .
I don't care what the weather's like. I know
About him. Don't put me off . . . O darling why
Pretend to happiness? You know I know . . .
Shut up! Shut up! Can anything I do
Ever get through your silly skull that he
Breathes up and laughs and coughs dishonesty,
Fat splayed cupidity, a walking lie,
Dumb cluck, a deadpan scrounger, any way
You find him out in . . . Hello . . . Hello . . .
    Goodbye . . .'

IV.
Who then are you
I hazard after?
Are you my love
Who have my love?
I cannot yet decipher you nor disprove.

Where do you lie
And what between

Us launches this arrogant
Atmosphere
Through which you penetrate like a pointed prayer?

I come to you
Across across,
I come to you
And will be seen
Though five ambiguous senses blaze between.

Just as the sun
Goes up and down
I come to you
Continually
Whether I circumambulate or climb high.

I move, I move.
I do not know
Where to nor why
Nor how except
That you are ahead of where my last step slept.

This wooden table
And this blue pen,
Tarmac, macadam
And turnstile are
On which your treadmarks glitter like a scar.

Waysiding with
Fellows and fools,
Or sidetracked by
Intelligence,
I come to you. I come through my ignorance.

In Arctic seas
Slack waters push
My path aside,
Yet I move through
Waves from far underwater and come to you.

My toe-tip on
A stiff arête
Topples a stone,
And as it falls
An echo of it murmurs. To you it calls.

A prison may
Cloister that noise,
Round four lean walls
Its echo grope,
But you, its audience, always interlope.

Down roads that I
Did not prefer,
Through rooms I hate,
Past doors I close,
I come to you for sustenance and repose.

My shadow swivels
Drunk and remorseful
Into the night
Against the kerb.
You are its nurse and you soothe it like an herb.

When I am divided
Into my last
Small share in the world
I have come through,
I would be broken like bread and come to you.

I come to you
Across across,
Across the street,
Across the years,
Come closer each breath as each breath disappears.

Along the edge
Of oceans and
Along the hedge's

Decorous side
I walk away out towards you and you abide.

Elusive and
Yet constant to
Constant pursuit;
To you, my remote
Last love, all my love that lasts, I must devote.

I cannot see
Smiles in another,
And every tear
I brush aside
I find you hidden within it like a bride.

Were you stargazing,
A shy ripple,
Facing the sky
You reconcile,
I'd come to you in disguise as your own smile.

Or were you moved
Against the mean
Earth we are made of,
I'd be the hand
You hilted anger with and your reprimand.

For where I go
It is I am carried
And the why of it all
Is you understand,
You my direction till you become my end.

Gently you make
Me move away
From whom I am
I was I will
Become, and gently return what I fulfil.

122

An obscure construction,
My final title,
Made to move
And carry the years
By law of you, a motley of engineers.

Yes, gently you,
My destination
Describe and limit
My life of loving
And listen as I come through the noise of moving.

I come to you
Across this painful
Noise of my journey
Without a wreath.
I bear no grudge nor cargo. I carry death.

You will surprise
Me at the last.
We two will meet
Where no sun warms,
I, murderer with my body in my arms,

And you with me
As I at last
With you, alive
Past apprehension,
The dizzy annunciation, the slackening tension.

June 1951—May 1952